ESCAPE INTO DANGER

ESCAPE INTO DANGER

by George Ivers

Illustrations by
George Ivers

CRITERION PRESS
CRANBURY, NEW JERSEY

Copyright © 1993 by George Ivers

All rights reserved. No part of this book may be copied, reproduced or used in any way without written permission of the publisher.

Printed in the United States of America

Cover by George Ivers

        Library of Congress Cataloging-in-Publication Data

Ivers, George, 1922-
    Escape into danger / by George Ivers : illustrations by George Ivers.
      p.   cm.
    ISBN 0-9638632-0-7 (pbk.) : $10.00
    1. Ivers, George, 1922- . 2. World War, 1939-1945–Prisoners and prisons, German. 3. World War, 1939-1945–Personal narratives, Polish. 4. Prisoners of war–Poland–Biography. 5. Prisoners of war–Spain–Biography. 6. Spain–History–Civil War, 1936-1939- -Personal narratives, Polish. 7. Escapes–Europe–History–20th century. I. Title.
D805.G3I85   1992
940.54'724332–dc20   93-34654
                                                                                                       CIP

Criterion Press
3A William Harrison Drive
Cranbury, NJ 08512

DEDICATION

This book was written for my dear sister Marysia; for my beloved wife, Iris; for my children, Stacy, Karen, Jeremy and Michael; for their children, Stephanie, Mike, Nicky and Jennifer; and for others yet to come.

I want to share it, also, with all my loving friends. I thank them for their encouragement. But, most of all, I want to thank my wonderful wife for her skillful and sensitive editing of my manuscript and for guiding me through the entire project.

TABLE OF CONTENTS

Foreword	xi
Rude Awakening	1
Taste of Seasalt	3
Bombshell	5
Death of a Songsparrow	9
POW	13
Bread Means Life	16
Mail from Home	18
Lousy Deal	20
Kazik and Janek	22
Felek	24
Sobish	26
Edek the Jeweler	28
Bread Crumbs and Blood	32
Rott Arbeits Commando	34
Escape	40
Runaway from Home	45
Recapture and Punishment	49
Penal Camp	54
Catacombs	57
Where is God?	60
Sinner	62
Poor Sobish	70
Yousek	72
Planning the Ruse	74

CONTENTS

Run for Your Life	78
Stealthy Hike	82
Midnight Bluff	84
Cornered	86
Night Hunter	88
Posse	90
Dead Man's Shoes	92
The Longest Day	93
Edge of Endurance	95
Shelter with Love	97
Last Stretch	101
The Finish Line	103
Oh, God, We Did It!	106
Licking Our Wounds	108
Secret Connection	110
Into France	113
Parting with Yousek	115
False Identity	119
Waiting	123
Spanish Sting	125
Dungeons of Spain	128
Miranda Concentration Camp	132
Life Behind the Walls	135
Some Tried	138
Tunnel	140
Hunger Strike	142
Yousek Again	144
Mail from Home	146
Madrid	149

CONTENTS

Sex Abuse at Four	153
Antelope	159
Gibraltar at Last	161
Captain Komorovski	164
S/S *Krosno*	170
Left in the Cold	175
Acceptance	178
The Wheel and the Compass	181
End of the War!	184
Shipless in London	187
Something in Common	189
The Letter	193
S/S *Bialystok*	195
Malted	199
Fight	201
Tempest	203
Christmas	206
Reserved Seat	222
Return	225
What My Parents Told Me	227
Writing on the Wall	235
Another Escape?	236
A New Beginning	238
Epilogue	241

FOREWORD

Perhaps someday I will be able to forgive, but I will never forget the German people for their war crimes.

I realize that a few opposed Nazism, but the German people as a whole idealized Adolf Hitler, seeing him as their savior. The enthusiasm exhibited at their open-air rallies was awesome. As I look at some of those old documentary films and at the multitudes screaming in unison, "*Sieg Heil!*" I am overcome with grief.

There will never be enough documentation to remind the world of Germany's vicious cruelty. That is why I wrote this book. During those days in the summer of 1940, when I was a 17-year-old POW in Germany, I solemnly promised myself two things: first, that when I would be free again, I'd eat a loaf of bread every day; and second, that I'd record by writing and drawing what I had experienced. The following is the fulfillment of that promise I made to myself over 50 years ago.

George Ivers
November 1992

RUDE AWAKENING

Weissenburg, Germany, June 1940

Where am I? I thought as I suddenly awoke. Am I having a nightmare? My mind was a squirming tangle of thoughts. The sharp glare of searchlights passing over my face every few minutes had awakened me. I shot up and found myself on a narrow, coffinlike bunk.

It was night, and the prison camp lay still. The searchlights atop the watchtowers scanned the barbed-wire fences, then glided along the prison walls, penetrating the interior where the prisoners slept. A moment later the lights slid off, and darkness again restored the order of the night. I sat still, dazed, not daring to accept reality.

Perhaps it *was* only a nightmare. I used to have

them as a child in Poland, and I remember waking up to the sound of my own screams of fright. But soon I would hear the soft-slippered footsteps of my mother approaching, and I calmed down at her reassuring whisper: "Don't be afraid, my little one. It's only a bad dream. Only a dream."

But this—this was real!

The room was cold and dim. A solitary light bulb at the end of the corridor failed to disperse the night shadows that hovered among the cramped, two-tiered bunks of raw wooden boards where men slept on bags of straw.

For many it was a tortured sleep, accentuated by spasms of coughing, heavy breathing and snoring. The odor of unwashed bodies, sweat and urine hung thick in the air.

How had I gotten here? What was happening to my world? It seemed that time suddenly had exploded and left in shambles my present and my future. Only a short while ago my star had burned brighter than I ever dreamed it would, and my future held the promise of adventure and success. I had graduated from high school just a few months before and had been accepted at the Polish Merchant Marine Academy, one of 14 lucky cadets chosen to take part in a training trip to South America.

At age 17, in smart uniforms, we were the envy of our peers. I felt the world was at my feet, ready for plucking.

I tried to sort out the events leading to my present predicament. I shut my eyes and thought about the day I left Poland.

TASTE OF SEASALT

It was a sunny July morning, and the air reverberated with the sounds of festive military marches as my ship, the *M/S Chrobry*, slowly inched away from the pier at Gdynia harbor on her maiden voyage to South America. Through a blizzard of confetti and colored streamers, I saw my father in the crowd of well-wishers, waving and mouthing those last indecipherable words of parental advice. A few minutes later I could barely distinguish his face as everything on shore grew smaller and smaller. At last a blast from the ship's bullhorn sounded a final good-bye.

   I wrote postcards home from every port, describing the sights and smells of a world that was opening up for me. Then at Buenos Aires we turned about and headed back for Poland. But as we reached Rio de Janeiro, our world suddenly collapsed. A strange and eerie excitement

ESCAPE INTO DANGER

swept over the ship. Men ran about in panic, shouting and questioning, as others tried to explain the news reports coming from the ship's radio room.

BOMBSHELL

Hitler's army had invaded Poland. Thousands had been killed in barbaric air strikes on the civilian population and Poland was falling to the Nazis. We were stunned. At first I didn't believe it. It must be a propaganda trick the Germans are playing on us, I thought. Since earliest childhood, I had been taught to believe that Poland was a powerful nation. How could it be that, in just a few short days, we on that ship had become people without a country, homeless wanderers? But as the hours passed, hope gave way to grim reality.

    I thought about my family and tried to imagine what they were going through. I saw my father, a tall, dark-haired man with a sweeping mustache, a respected schoolmaster, and my loving mother, also a teacher. Would they have to hide from the Germans or run for their lives? My older sister, Viesia, was a medical student in Poznan. She would probably join the Resistance and help with the wounded. My younger sister, Marysia, was only 13. Thinking of her, I felt guilty for not having shown her enough of my love. I also felt terribly guilty that fate had removed me so neatly from the war zone, and that I was living in comparative safety while my family agonized every day—if, indeed, they were still alive.

My only passion—a burning, all-consuming one—was to find a way to join either the English or French forces and fight the Nazis.

Meanwhile, the sea around us bristled with hostile activity. The German battleship *Graf Spee*, with her flotilla of support ships, controlled the South Atlantic. However, despite all the dangers, our ship managed to zigzag her way safely to England.

There my group of classmates quickly melted away. Some went to the United States to live with relatives. Others continued their studies in English schools.

"And what are you going to do, Yurek (my nickname)?" asked one of my friends, who had already enlisted in a Polish division that was forming in France.

"I'm going to fight, too," I said, "but I want to join an outfit that will put me directly into combat." A short time later, I joined a Polish reconnaissance unit, and early in the winter of 1940 I shipped to France.

Polish volunteers from all over arrived to join the 1st Grenadiers Division that was forming in Coetquidan, in northern France, under the command of Polish General Duch. This Polish division was incorporated into the French army under the supreme command of General Gamelin.

Despite the cold winter of 1940 and inadequate housing conditions, the spirit in the camp was very high. Coetquidan was a small town in the province of Brittany. It resembled a refugee center, with many civilians, as well as soldiers, all waiting for assignments, uniforms, equipment. The French government issued us soldiers outdated World War I uniforms, and we looked like extras on a movie set.

By a strange coincidence, I was assigned to a reconnaissance unit commanded by a captain who had the very same name as I, Jerzy Iwaszkiewicz (my name before I Americanized it years later). He was middle-aged and looked and sounded tough. He had left Poland long before the war started, coming to France and serving as an officer in the French Foreign Legion. One day I was told to report to him. He was mildly pleasant and asked me about my relatives. It turned out that we were distant cousins. (Later the sameness of our names would play an important role in my escape from the Nazis.) When he asked my age, I told him I was 17. "Soldier," I remember him snapping, "you must learn to shoot well. War is no fun." As the days went by, I felt he avoided any closeness despite our family ties, and he never called me by my first name.

Target shooting was our main activity day after day. The Hotchkiss-type machine guns often jammed and were slow in firing. So here we were, with outdated equipment, yet with soaring spirits.

This was not the first time Poles had joined the French to fight the Germans. The last had been during World War I, when Polish soldiers under the command of French General Haller marched the same roads, sang the same songs and used the same quarters. Later on, we would notice Polish names carved into barn rafters in many of the villages, including those in the Vosges Mountains and Lorraine.

Several celebrities were in our ranks, older men with graying hair who, despite their age, wanted to fight the Nazis. They served with us as ordinary soldiers. Among them were Joseph Lipski, the Polish ambassador to Berlin; Jan Rembielinski, a Polish senator; and the author and writer R. Siemienski. We also had some defenders of

Warsaw who had escaped to France, and some Poles who had escaped from Russian labor camps, where they had been sent as soon as the Russian army occupied their part of Poland. These volunteers had traveled thousands of miles to join the Polish Grenadiers division that was forming in France.

Finally, in April 1940, we were shipped in freight trains to Lorraine, near Luxemburg. This was the war zone, and here we set up our defenses.

But soon after, we learned the depressing news that the Germans had overtaken and occupied Holland and Belgium. A few weeks later, Hitler reached for Paris. The French air force was annihilated on the ground. General Gamelin proved to be incompetent and was replaced by General Veigand. The Germans moved toward Paris, encountering almost no resistance. In the meantime, our Polish division covered the backs of the retreating French army.

DEATH OF A SONGSPARROW

At 17, I was the youngest soldier in my company. My assignments varied from minute to minute. Sometimes I carried crates of ammunition for machine guns; at other times, I was a messenger. As we dug wide ditches for the entrapment of German tanks, we were overwhelmed by the rapidity of their advance. Every day we were under attack from the German Luftwaffe. Chaos, fear and exhaustion marked each moment as we retreated, trying to shelter the French army. Many of my comrades were killed or wounded.

Events occurred in such rapid succession that now I can only remember chaotic flashes, without any logical sequence:

ESCAPE INTO DANGER

Three dark objects break off from the blue June sky and in seconds become three German Stuka airplanes. One of them dives with a terrifying whine. It comes straight for me as I run for shelter in a garden ditch, my heart pounding. The plane is so close I can see the goggled face of the pilot. Barely aiming, I fire my rifle, then hug the ground. A bomb suddenly explodes only a few feet away. The impact is deafening. Acrid smoke billows in a dark gray cloud that fills my nostrils and chokes me. In seconds, which seem to stretch into eternity, debris starts falling all around me. I feel chunks of earth hitting my back. Terrified, I think I have been hit by fragments of the bomb. I moan, more in fright than in pain. Huddled down and not daring to move, I see from the corner of my eye the still smoking bomb crater. Suddenly the plane returns with a shrill, piercing howl. It splatters a trail of machine-gun bullets, missing me by only a few yards. I try to move but can't. Within my arm's reach, I notice a dead songsparrow, pierced by a piece of twig.

*   *   *

It is a hot June day. I am with the company commander at the edge of a woods. He looks through his binoculars into the valley, where our men with heavy machine guns lie entrenched in a cemetery. Ahead of them, barely visible, German mobile mortar artillery units advance. Soon they are laying on a barrage of fire, cutting off the escape route from the cemetery. I hear the whining of bullets; shrapnel bursts closer to us with every passing minute. The commander curses loudly, ducks into a foxhole and yells at me: "Soldier, you are to deliver a message to Lieutenant Polanski to withdraw immediately eastward and rendezvous with the trucks in the village! Run like hell, soldier!" I am sure I'll be hit this time, trying to get through this barrage. I run like mad. I hear the whistling of missiles all around me. I hit the ground and lie flat for a few seconds, then run again. I see the green turf of the meadow being torn up, as if ripped by powerful claws, and immediately replaced by scars of smoldering black tar. I keep falling as I run downward toward the cemetery. Before I realize it, I am already there. I yell my message, and the men move out immediately. Then I am running back up the hill. The hot June sun is beating down mercilessly. I wish I could shed my heavy overcoat, but I am hopelessly strapped in with a belt and other military paraphernalia. I turn around and see German soldiers advancing behind panzer tanks, which keep sending blasts of fire in our direction. I trip and fall, and while getting up I notice some beautiful, ripe strawberries. It is strange what one remembers. I quickly stuff some into my mouth. Finally I scramble over a stone-wall fence and clear the crest. Once on even ground, I run toward our trucks. The village is now under artillery fire, and the trucks have started to move out. I yell, and one slows down. With enormous effort, I grab the tailgate, and the hands of my companions pull me in.

*   *   *

The woods look like a garbage dump. Strewn everywhere are parts of uniforms, equipment, office files, piles of paper—as if a hurricane had swept through. There is an ambulance smashed against a tree. Through its open door, gleaming surgical instruments have spilled onto the forest floor. An overpowering stench drifts up from an area where I can see dead horses distended like big dark balloons, their stiff legs pointing toward the blue sky. And in that sky a German plane circles slowly, scattering a cloud of leaflets that call for the surrender of the French army. Disbelieving, we watch the French soldiers lay down their arms in great piles. Many of them have deserted their units and roam

ESCAPE INTO DANGER

around, drunk and disheveled, kicking their helmets and chanting: "La guerre est finis." What irony! We are trying to defend France, which does not want to be defended.

*   *   *

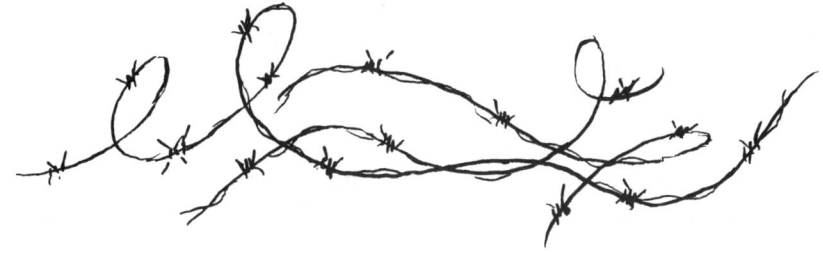

POW

Finally, on June 21, 1940, the Germans closed the noose in the valley of Saint Dié, and the French army, including my Polish division of Grenadiers, became hopelessly entrapped. We were like flies caught in a Nazi cobweb.

The hot sun showed no mercy as we prisoners marched three abreast in a seemingly endless column, escorted by our German guards. Their tanks clattered along, menacing us with their mighty guns. We walked for days without food. At night we were herded into barbed-wire enclosures. In the morning, as the guards screamed and cursed, we resumed the march. Finally, we arrived at a large POW camp in Weissenburg, Germany, just across the French border. . . .

As I lay on my sack of straw, with the night winding

down, I felt I had finally bridged the memory gap from that July morning, just a year before, when I left Poland. A pale gray dawn was slowly diluting the darkness. The uncertain light of morning reflected the hopeless gloom of the camp, and the searchlights stopped their tireless spying. I also stopped my thoughts from searching the past.

I was just about to fall asleep again when the sudden shrill blast of whistles and the curses of the capos turned the morning stillness into mad, hellish activity. The prisoners quickly got up and scrambled to wash at the few spigots of running water, or dashed for the latrines. A line had already formed for a cup of ersatz tea as the shrieks of whistles sounded again, this time announcing roll call.

We stood shivering a long time in the morning chill while the head count took place. The camp commandant paraded in front of the formation, then stopped and delivered a speech filled with vitriol and contempt. His words were translated by a prisoner-interpreter, who mimicked the inflections of the commander's lecture on the supremacy of the Third Reich. Then some prisoners were chosen for work details outside the camp. These were envied jobs, because they presented an opportunity for acquiring some extra bread and other foodstuffs that could be smuggled into the camp, where food rations were so meager that prisoners were often starving.

Living so close to the bottom of existence, even the smallest shreds of security become extremely important in the process of survival. Surreptitiously, deals were made with some of the guards, who would swap a loaf of bread for a watch or a ring or anything of value. Some of the prisoners were very crafty. Others had been professional jewelers, tailors or cabinet makers, and the guards would often reward them for their handiwork. The daily ration of bread became a symbol of life, because without it one would surely perish.

POW

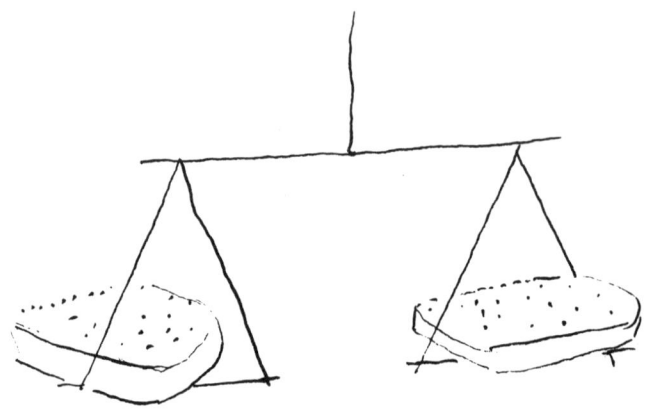

BREAD MEANS LIFE

The bread was distributed in the evenings, each loaf shared by eight very hungry men. The dividing of the bread became a ritual that, even after so many years, refuses to leave my memory.

A makeshift scale was constructed of cardboard and string. The bread was carefully cut, then each slice weighed individually and measured against the others. I remember the ring of eight men standing closely around a table, watching with burning eyes every crumb that tipped the scale, their outstretched fingers, clawlike, ready to grab. I remember the salivating mouths, the bared teeth frantic to bite, the throats swallowing hard in anticipation.

I also remember the early days of captivity when no bread had been issued for several days. One day a truck loaded with green, moldy bread arrived at the gate. Prisoners were detailed to strip off the moldy parts, which were then placed on an old blanket, sprayed with chlorine and dumped into latrine trenches. I was sick with dysentery then, squatting on planks that had been laid across such a trench. My intestines were bleeding, and I was in a bad way with fever and weakness. And I remember seeing starving men scavenge for those filthy, moldy, chlorine-spotted bits of bread in those latrine trenches.

Hunger is difficult to understand, no matter how well it is described. In order to comprehend it fully, one must experience it. And even then, after being well fed again, it is so easy to forget how it really felt. I remember solemnly vowing that, if I ever got out of that place alive, I would eat a loaf of bread every day! And I also cursed myself for my stupidity in not having done so before I was captured.

MAIL FROM HOME

One day the Germans issued mail cards to the prisoners so that we could write to our families. These were form cards, and we were told we could write only a few lines and that only positive statements would be allowed. My immediate reaction was not to write. What if this were a trick, a way to learn of the whereabouts of our relatives in Poland? Would the Germans take advantage of such information and punish my family for any deeds they had done?

I agonized over this. Finally, after much deliberation, I decided to risk it. I certainly didn't expect to get an answer. Yet, incredibly, after a few weeks I received a form letter from my father. He assured me that they were all well and very happy to hear from me. And they were still living in our home.

MAIL FROM HOME

After a while prisoners started to receive packages, and one day I received one, too. Unfortunately, the Germans confiscated all the foodstuffs, but they did leave me some underwear, a toothbrush and soap.

The letters that I was allowed to receive once a month lifted my spirits immeasurably. I looked at my father's neat, almost calligraphic handwriting and felt reassured. I dreamed of my return and the ways we would all tell our stories, trying to fill in the gaps for each other.

In the meantime, I evaluated the serious situation I was in and how I was wasting away my young life in this forsaken prison camp. From the very beginning of my capture, I had decided that I would break out at the first reasonable opportunity. However, this would not be easy. The camp was well guarded, and the high fences constructed of barbed wire. Machine guns atop the two towers could cut down anyone approaching the fence. And just outside the gate, a German guard marched back and forth, holding a mean-looking dog on a leash. I knew it would be very difficult, if not impossible, to escape from there. My hope was that I might be selected for a work detail outside the camp. Meanwhile, I observed very carefully and kept my eyes and ears open.

LOUSY DEAL

After morning roll call, the prisoners would mill around the camp area. One day I sat down against the dormitory wall with my friend Janek. We had taken off our shirts and were killing the lice and lice nits that bred in the seams. As we pounded the shirts with a flat rock, I could sometimes feel a louse pop. Oh, how I hated lice! Perhaps more, even, than hunger itself. There was no way to protect yourself. In the dormitories, they crawled from one body to another. At first you hardly knew the louse was feeding on you. Then, as you felt a persistent itch, you finally realized it was eating you alive. Cursing, I threw down the rock and popped them with the flat of my fingernail into a squishy mess. Then I scraped the seams with a piece of wood, trying to get rid of the dead parasites.

LOUSY DEAL

The time came when the Germans brought a delousing steam-boiler unit to the camp. We were told to strip and waited naked in a slow-moving line while our hair was clipped and our heads swathed with some awful stinking disinfectant. Meanwhile, our belongings were steam boiled. This treatment proved to be effective for a limited time only.

At other times, laundering one's garments was both difficult and risky—difficult because it was not easy to get either water or a container in which to carry it, and there was virtually no soap. The risk involved the timing of doing such a wash. If my garment did not dry before the next roll call, I would have to stand shivering in the winter cold without my shirt, which would still be drying back on my bunk. Luckily, I had my long army coat in such an emergency.

There was a big potbelly stove in the dormitory, and everyone tried to get close to it to dry his laundry or just to warm up. But the stove was controlled by Ivan, a big square-shouldered Neanderthal. An illiterate Ukrainian peasant, Ivan hated most of the prisoners and wouldn't allow them to get close to the fire. He was so intimidating that no one ever tried to confront him physically. On the contrary, some even offered him a piece of bread for the privilege of drying their clothes. If Ivan disliked you, he would push you away with powerful hands as big as frying pans. His short, stubby neck ended abruptly in a bullet-shaped head, and he stooped forward like a gorilla. In the hollows under his massive brow gleamed bestial little eyes. I avoided him, especially after an incident when he tangled with me while I was trying to dry my shirt. He swung me around with such force that I lost my balance and hit the stove with my head. I blacked out for a while and blood gushed from where my head had been cut. From then on, I was very careful.

KAZIK AND JANEK

Kazik Bielski, who bunked just a few rows from me, was a talented singer. He had a fine, heart-tugging tenor voice, and at times he sang sentimental Polish songs. One day a German officer heard him. "Where did you learn to sing so well?" the officer asked.

"In the Warsaw Conservatory of Music," Kazik lied. "I also performed in the Warsaw Opera Palace."

"Then you know operas! That's marvelous!" exclaimed the officer, clearly delighted. "You will perform at the officers club next week."

Once dismissed, Kazik was distraught. "I know the melodies," he told us, "but I don't know the Italian words."

"Don't worry," Janek Volski said, trying to calm him down. Janek was our language expert, having taught that subject at Paderewski High School in Poznan. "We'll just make up words to some famous arias. I'll bet the Krauts will never know the difference. With your voice, you'll be a sensation." So in the days that followed, between roll calls, Kazik and Janek worked feverishly, and Kazik's voice could be heard reverberating throughout the barracks. The language, however, was very strange—a mixture of Polish, Latin and Italian. Kazik came from Warsaw and was actually a taxi driver. Tall, dark and handsome, he could easily fit the image of an opera singer, particularly if performing before a less-than-sophisticated audience.

After his performance, the payoff was immediate. Kazik was told to report to the gate. There he was given two loaves of bread and some cheese. We all ate well that night.

FELEK

Felek, Sobish and I had all been seamen when the war started. Felek had been a waiter on the luxury liner *S/S Pilsudski*. Like most of us, he was frightfully thin and thought constantly of food. His expressive eyes reflected the vibrant personality of an actor, but his dreams of going on stage had never materialized. Sometimes, though, he would use his dramatic style of speaking to entertain us and help us deal with the long nights.

"Hey, Felek," someone would say, "tell us again about the food you dumped overboard!"

And so Felek, warming to his subject, would be off, describing the lavishness of the cuisine on board the cruise ship. "Sure, there were times when I dumped cornish hens and veal cutlets overboard. The stupid guests

FELEK

kept changing their orders, and I wasn't going to face the chef with all those corrections. He wouldn't like it one bit. It was easier to dump the whole order over the side, plates and all."

"Couldn't you hide it somewhere?" someone hungrily inquired.

"There was no time for such things", Felek replied, impatiently. "Besides, what would I do with it? I had more food than I could ever eat." Felek's voice trailed off. He seemed lost in memories. When he spoke again, his voice was warm and rich. "When I served dinner," he said, "the first thing I'd bring would be a tray of golden melon adorned with delicate slices of prosciutto ham. Then the soup—the favorite was Consomme Varsovien. Then crusty warm loaves of Italian bread drenched in garlic butter and sprinkled with finely chopped parsley or chives. . . ."

At this point Felek was usually told by someone: "Shut up or I'll kill you!" while others begged for more. Ironically, it was the prison camp that provided Felek with an opportunity to display his acting talent.

SOBISH

Sobish, a short, stocky man of 30 with a rusty beard, had been a boatswain on a Polish tramp freighter. He had sailed all over the world in command of his deck crew. His deep baritone voice and no-nonsense bearing brought him attention and respect whenever he spoke. I tried to imagine what Sobish was like when dealing with his crew. The man had to be super tough to order those boisterous and unruly seamen around. In the prison camp he seldom spoke, but when he did no one would argue with him.

One evening, after standing in the wet snow at roll call, my feet felt like ice, and as soon as I got back to the barracks I went close to the stove to dry my shoes. Ivan was there and resented it. He grabbed me by the throat, cursing me in a foul way. Luckily, Sobish was nearby, and he shouted at Ivan to let me go. Ivan released me, then turned on Sobish as the latter shouted, "You're a dirty sonofabitch bastard!" Then Sobish shoved his knee in Ivan's groin. Ivan howled like a wounded dog. The next moment someone grabbed an overcoat and threw it over Ivan's head. Then 10 pairs of hands seized him. It was like trying to wrestle Gulliver, but Ivan went down with a terrible crash. I'm sure he never forgot the beating he got. From then on, he didn't bother anyone at the stove, and I was grateful to Sobish.

As time went by, a group of us became friends, sharing food and helping each other in various emergencies.

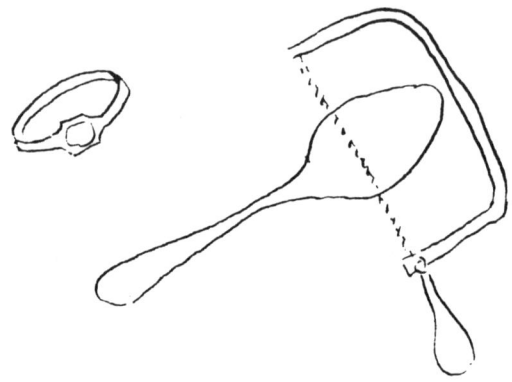

EDEK THE JEWELER

Escape was an all-consuming thought, always on my mind. As I watched my body deteriorate into skin and bones, I knew I had to act soon, while I was still strong enough to run. But it was winter, and I feared the piercing cold and the possibility of being shot. I looked down at my enormous, bony knees and almost fleshless thighs covered with scabs from scratching lice. My fears dissolved into rage. I thought of my youth and of how, at 18, my life was beginning to end. I was rapidly expiring at the hands of these hated oppressors, and I knew that I *must* escape.

Since my capture, I had experienced many emotional upheavals. My initial fear and depression had given way to a festering and gnawing anger. I fingered a small metal ID tag around my neck that bore the name of the camp and my

EDEK THE JEWELER

POW number, 11091. A row of perforations ran across the middle. I realized the perforations had a sinister purpose. If something should happen to me, the tag could be broken in two. Half would go with my body and the other half into a record file. The Germans were known for keeping meticulous records of anything that could be counted.

I felt it would be an outrage if I should perish there, unnoticed, forgotten, with no one to care, simply becoming a statistic. I had too many rich and beautiful expectations for myself, and I had just begun to live. I felt severed from my family and friends, and abandoned by God. No, I would not let this happen to me! In order to survive, I knew I had to become a cunning fox and that I could depend on no one but myself.

One evening I was talking to Edek, a young man I had befriended. Edek had been a jeweler. He was known in the camp for creating beautiful rings, using whatever materials were available, mostly spoons. Edek was in his mid-20s and had flaxen hair and sad, gray eyes. He was a very quiet man. One day I asked him, "Edek, how did you happen to get here, so far from Poland?"

He thought for a while and then replied, "It's a long story. I lived in Lvov, and during the early days of the war the Russians came to our town. They sent me and many others to a labor camp far into Russia. But later, when Hitler got after the Russkies, I managed to get to Iran, then to Gibraltar, and finally to France. There I joined the Polish division. You know the rest." He grimaced as he polished a ring he had just finished making.

A few days later Edek confided in me. "Listen, Yurek," he said. "I've got to get out of here. I can't stand this prison camp anymore. Not only am I missing the best part of my life, but I'm scared I'm going to die here. You see, there is something wrong with my lungs. I keep coughing and spitting up blood." I listened in awe as he talked that way. "If I have to die," he continued, "I might just as well make a break for it. What I'm saying is, will you go with me?"

"Edek," I answered, "the thought of escape is always on my mind—has been since the first day I was captured." Without hesitation, I continued, "If your plan is good, I'll go with you."

"Don't talk to anyone about it," he whispered. "First we have to get picked for an outside work detail. That's the only way, because the camp is too well guarded."

I looked around to see if anyone was listening and then said, "Maybe you could trade a ring with a guard and ask him to select us."

"Good idea," Edek agreed, slapping me on the back.

During the following days Edek tried to strike a deal. Finally, one morning he told me, "It's on for today. I spoke with a guard, and he liked the ring. He told me to wait at the front gate right after morning roll call. So stick around me, and we'll both get picked."

As we stood at the gate, the guard came with a work list. Edek and I were already counted in when suddenly a sergeant walked over, looked at the list, rechecked the count and then pushed me into another work group. There was nothing I could do as I watched Edek and a few dozen others climb onto an open truck. The driver started the engine, and the truck picked up speed as it passed the gatehouse and headed down the road.

I found myself in Rott arbeits commando group. We had to march to our work site three abreast, with guards on both sides of the column. All day I thought of Edek and could hardly wait until evening to talk to him.

That night we both expressed disappointment at our separation, but he told me he was determined to break out anyway. "You see," he said, "at one point the road turns sharply and the truck has to slow down. Some woods are nearby. There are only three guards for about 20 men. We stand in the truck, holding on to the sides and each other, and the guards lean against the driver's cab, watching us. I think I could jump off at the slow turn and, before the truck could stop or the guards start shooting, I could reach the woods."

"My God, Edek!" I gasped. "I hope you know what you're doing! You'd better figure out every step carefully."

We talked in hushed voices. I felt the excitement of his impending escape, but I also felt envious and frightened. "It's too bad we got separated," he said again, "but I must do it anyway. It'll take some time to figure out every detail before I go."

I couldn't sleep that night. Again the searchlights from the watchtowers lit up my face every few minutes, as if saying: *Are you still here?*

BREAD CRUMBS AND BLOOD

I was in the last row of the three-abreast column of my work detail. The guards walked along on both sides, 10 guards for 50 prisoners. As we marched, I tried to make eye contact with the civilians who were watching us from windows and doorways. There were many French living in Alsace. A number of them hated the Germans and called them *Boche*. I wished they would give us some food. We were starving. That's why I had positioned myself last on the right side of the column, close to the sidewalk. Someone had once told me that, if you were last, no one could see you from the front, and sometimes a passerby might offer you some bread. If only one guard saw it, he might look the other way as long as no other guards were watching.

BREAD CRUMBS AND BLOOD

Whoever told me that was at least partially right, for one day I noticed a pleasant-looking middle-aged woman with a little girl, perhaps six years old, walking toward us and getting closer to me with every step. The woman carried a bulging shopping bag and held the little girl by the hand. Just as the woman got very close to me, she pulled a beautiful, round loaf of bread from her bag. I could smell the delicious aroma of the freshly baked sourdough. The woman and child stopped. The little girl was now holding the bread in both her small hands, and she offered it to me. I could hardly believe my luck. In one swift motion, I snatched the bread, and then . . . all hell broke loose! As if they had eyes in the back of their heads, suddenly all the prisoners knew! They swarmed all over me, attacking me with what seemed like hundreds of sharp claws from a flock of predatory birds. I was knocked to the ground and the bread smashed into pieces. As I lay there flat on my back, someone tried to pry open my fists in search of some bread, but I didn't have any.

They tore at my shirt and scratched my face. They bit each other like animals. Amid curses from the guards and shrieks of pain from the prisoners, everyone tumbled about in a frenzy. In a way, I was protected by the bodies of my desperate companions on top of me, who were suddenly receiving a beating from the guards. Their rifle butts crushed the skeletal bodies of the prisoners, whose blood gushed and leaked down all over me as I lay on the ground. Within minutes, the column reassembled and we marched on, leaving behind on the roadway small piles of bread crumbs drenched in blood.

ROTT ARBEITS COMMANDO

Once we reached the work site of Rott arbeits commando, the men were divided into small groups and given shovels and picks. Our job was to clear the area, which was littered with debris from artillery bombardments. The debris was mostly bricks, rocks and chunks of buildings that had been destroyed. It was back-breaking work, picking up those heavy chunks and carrying them to another site. We toiled like Egyptian slaves building the pyramids. It was still winter, and a cold wind blew right through our thin clothing. The guards built a fire from wood debris and warmed themselves while we worked. At noon a whistle blew, and we lined up for soup. As I stood in front of two big steaming field kettles, I sent the orderly my strongest thoughts: Ladle my soup from deep down near the bottom where a potato or a turnip might be hiding. Yet it was always the same murky liquid, with barely the shadow of a cabbage leaf. I slurped it hungrily from my tin can.

Because it was the lunch hour, prisoners dragged in scraps of wood and started a fire of their own. We bunched around it and talked, wishing it were summer. "Wouldn't it be nice," someone said, "not to freeze anymore. And by then, the war might be over. If only America would join in against Germany. But the Yankees are playing it safe, not realizing that, sooner or later, they'll have to declare war against Hitler. In the meantime, he's growing fatter and fatter." Speculation went on and on, till a whistle blew and the guards yelled at us to get busy.

One day in the late afternoon I happened to overhear an argument between an engineering official and the German lieutenant in charge of our work site. I put my high school German to work and was able to fathom the nature of the disagreement. Then I heard the lieutenant holler: "You mean to tell me there is no one here who speaks both German and Polish? How the hell can you make these men understand what they're supposed to do?" At that point he turned around to us and yelled: "Does anyone here speak Deutsch?"

I was ready for that, and I said: "*Ich spreche Deutsch, Herr Lieutenant.*"

"Ah, goot!" he exclaimed. "You, then, are now in charge of the prisoner lists and the sites they are to be assigned. You'll stay in the office with Herr Hoffner."

"*Jawohl, Herr Lieutenant,*" I replied smartly.

I was both delighted and scared. I would be out of the cold. And no more back-breaking labor. But I was afraid they'd find out how little German I really knew.

Back at the camp I told Edek about my luck and added that now I'd have a better chance to break out, since I wouldn't be watched so closely. "Lucky you," he said. "I wish it were me. It looks like a great opportunity."

ESCAPE INTO DANGER

The next morning at roll call I assisted with the work assignments. My companions regarded me with envy. Then I was escorted to the office of the building engineer, which was in a little house near the camp. There I was told to sit at a small table on which I placed my lists. I was very frightened but tried not to show it. Frankly, I didn't know what I was supposed to do. So I shifted my papers, pretending to be busy, and read them over and over. At the other end of the room, behind a large desk piled high with ledgers and papers, sat Herr Hoffner. Out of the corner of my eye, I watched his taciturn face.

Herr Hoffner was in his 30s and was probably a rather short man, though I never saw him stand. He had a club foot, and that had probably kept him out of the army. His armband with the Nazi swastika, however, clearly bespoke his allegiance, and his square, swarthy face, framed with black, carefully combed and well-greased hair, never betrayed emotion. I didn't ever succeed in making eye contact with him, and he rarely spoke to me. However, I knew that he was responsible for me, and that he watched me very carefully.

I would often excuse myself to go to the toilet, in order to carefully observe my new environment. The lavatory had a door that locked. High up was a small window, which overlooked a narrow alley. The rest of the house was occupied by a middle-aged woman, probably French Alsatian. I felt that her sentiments were anti-Nazi, because at times she left a boiled potato or scraps of food for me, in a cat dish, on the floor near the lavatory. One day she waited for me and motioned toward the dish. Of course, she was forbidden to give food to the prisoners, and this way she felt safe.

After a few days I devised a plan. I decided I'd slip out through the lavatory window, cross the road and vanish into the woods. Then I'd walk south to Switzerland. That should take about two weeks. Carefully I saved my bread rations, relying now only on the cat-dish leftovers put there for me by this kind woman.

The idea of breaking out frightened me, and I was on the verge of panic. I imagined myself being hunted down by Nazi soldiers.

One evening after roll call Edek walked over to me and whispered, "I want to say good-bye to you. Tomorrow at this time I'll be gone. I've checked all the possibilities. Jumping off the truck on the return trip is the best time. It'll be getting dark then."

"Well, Edek," I said, "I wish you luck. And I'll tell you something. I've decided to break out, too, as soon as I can," and I told him my plan.

"See you in England," he said.

We shook hands and embraced for only a second, so as not to attract attention.

So this is it, I thought. Tomorrow night there will be a lot of talk here about Edek's escape. I could hardly wait until then. When five o'clock approached I felt some of the excitement and fear that Edek was probably experiencing. It had started to rain, then turned to sleet. Finally, after what seemed an eternity, his group arrived back at camp.

"Something's wrong," someone shouted. "The Krauts are keeping them at the gate." I heard fragments of other conversations:

"What's going on? Someone must be sick."

"Look! They're carrying someone."

"The whole detail has been detained for questioning."

"There's been an escape attempt. Someone was shot. Who was it?"

My heart sank. It was obvious that Edek hadn't made it, but was he still alive?

When the work detail was finally dismissed and got back to our barracks, we heard the whole story. "Edek hadn't told anyone of his plan," one of the fellows on the truck told us, "so when the truck slowed down at a sharp turn, we couldn't believe our eyes. He just jumped off! It had started sleeting and we were going real slow. The guards saw him right away, and they banged on the driver's cab to stop. We saw Edek running for his life into the woods. The guards screamed at everyone to get out. '*Raus! Raus!*' they shrieked. 'Lie down, everyone!' We lay prone on our bellies. One guard watched us with his gun at the ready. Out of the corner of my eye I saw two other guards, each kneeling, aiming at Edek. We heard several shots. It was getting dark. Good, I thought. This will help him. But, no, his number was up. I heard one guard yell out: 'I've got him!' They ordered two of us to get up and bring him back. When we saw him, he was dying. He moved his lips and his eyes glazed over. Blood was pouring from his back. In a moment he was still and limp. We carried him to the truck." The man was so distraught he could barely continue. "What I can't understand," he sobbed, "is that the same guard who killed Edek had given him a piece of bread earlier that day."

Terrible grief choked my throat. I could still hear Edek's last words to me: "*See you in England.*" And then I thought, What if we had been together? Maybe *I* would have gotten the bullet.

I couldn't sleep that night. Again the searchlights seemed to say: *You are next if you try. We'll get you next.*

The following morning was Sunday, our day off. No work details. It was the day we licked our wounds. However, we still had roll call, and the blasts of the whistles got everyone out. As we lined up, four men were selected and told to go to the gate. They were to pick up a stretcher with a bluish-gray body on it, the body of Edek. Then they were ordered to parade the stretcher in front of our line-up.

Herr Hauptman Otto Richter, the camp commandant, strutted in front of us like a peacock, whipping his shiny, equestrian boots with a leather quirt as his long, elegant leather coat gleamed in the frosty morning. The fact that he was present conveyed a message of dangerous importance. The Polish interpreter, Kmiecik, translated his speech, imitating Richter's arrogant tone and his shrieks of wrath and insults. "Let this be a warning to you," he shouted. "You will be shot on sight if you try to escape! You dummy Polacken! You will work here for the Third Reich till the war is over. We are winning on all fronts. So you can see that there is no place for you to run! Now you can see for yourself if it pays to try. You are ordered to look at your comrade, Edward Bachmaciuk. Anyone not looking will be severely punished."

Then the pallbearers carried poor Edek's body in front of each row. I heard men sobbing as they looked at him. When they got close to me, I choked up and felt my whole body shaking. Mentally I kept repeating my worst curses: *You fucking shit bastards! You fucking Krauts! You'll pay for this!* On the outside I clenched my teeth so hard I thought my jaws would crack, and I stared at Edek's body. Not so with Janek, who stood next to me. You stupid asshole, I thought. Keep your eyes on him! But no. As the stretcher approached, I saw the guards watching everyone, trying to spot someone who couldn't bear to look. Janek gagged and turned his head. In a second it was too late. One of the guards slammed his rifle butt right between Janek's eyes. Blood spattered as he fell, moaning, to his knees. By then the guards were already nailing someone else. I kept standing still as a ramrod. Janek was still on his knees.

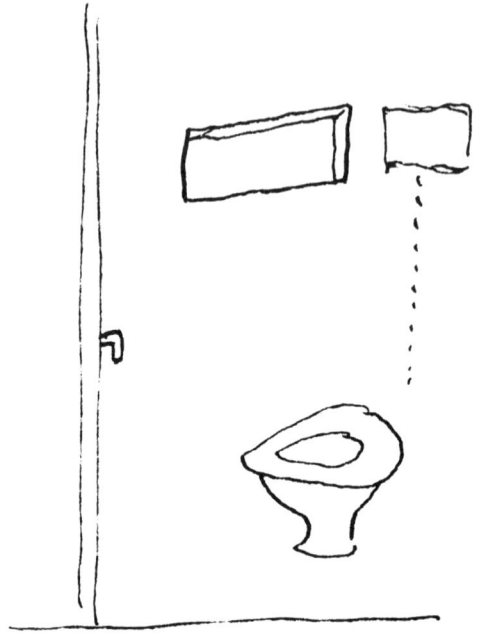

ESCAPE

For the time being, I considered myself extremely fortunate to be spared hard physical labor and given the chance to lick out the cat's bowl. I could probably survive the war quite well if this situation continued indefinitely.

But just surviving was not enough for me. I wanted to be active, part of the force that would punish the Nazis. I wanted to see them crumble and choke on their Aryan pride. I wanted to see their arrogant faces slapped, and see fear in their eyes.

Then again . . . it would be so easy to drop all my escape plans, plans that would surely place my life in jeopardy.

The window was small and high enough to be overlooked by the guards as an escape route. On my frequent visits to the toilet, I measured my possibilities carefully. While standing on the toilet seat, I tried to pull myself up and into the window. Unfortunately, the seat was too low. If only I had something to stand on, I thought. One day I noticed the door to the utility room half open. Inside was a small wooden crate just perfect for my purpose. The next day the door was closed, but when I tried the handle it opened easily. I realized that it wasn't kept locked, and that I would probably be able to get the crate when I needed it.

The only way I could get through the window was head first. This worried me, because I would have to get my legs out before I could let go of the window frame, and if I failed I would drop 10 feet down on my head. Again and again I mentally went through the motions of this operation and discovered that I'd be able to brace myself with one hand extended against the wall of the house next door, which was about three feet away. Then I would descend like a spider.

I went over every detail of this plan many times until I was sure I would be able to do it mechanically, without thinking. Thinking and anticipating all this made me sick with nausea. I could not allow any emotions to interfere with my plans.

On the day I was to escape, I told Herr Hoffner that I had an upset stomach. I wanted him to get used to my frequent and lengthy trips to the lavatory. I didn't have to fake this because I actually was sick with fear. Finally, in the afternoon, I made my last trip.

On the way to the toilet I opened the door to the utility room and took the crate. I locked myself in the lavatory and stuffed the keyhole with a piece of rag. That would give me a few precious minutes should Herr Hoffner try to open the door. Within seconds I had set the crate on the toilet seat and pulled myself up to the window. As I hung out through it, I braced myself against the neighboring building, pulled my legs through and quickly dropped into the narrow alley. In a few moments, I reached the corner and, with my heart pounding, quickly crossed the road. Luckily, no one was around. I crossed to the other side. Once in the underbrush and trees, I ran deep into the woods.

In a short while I became aware that someone must have noticed me, probably a civilian, because I heard gunshots. Civilians were paid rewards for the recapture of prisoners. I heard someone yell, then what sounded like a stampede and a pounding of boots. I ran madly for my life, as if I were a rabbit being chased by hunters, and, like a rabbit, I sidetracked and dove into a clump of dense bushes surrounding a large oak tree. There I lay, motionless, half covered by dry leaves and the low branches of young hemlocks.

I heard heavy boots racing by, but I didn't dare look. It turned out that the oak tree above me was a roosting place for large black crows, which, now alarmed, flapped their wings and filled the air with frantic shrieks. This unusual commotion by the birds attracted some of the village boys, who ran over and started throwing stones at the crows. I prayed they'd soon be called home to supper. I lay there motionless for a long time.

Eventually the boys left, day became night and the woods fell silent. Very, very carefully I crawled from my hiding place. Immediately I felt a burning pain in my hip. I must have banged into a tree in my mad flight. But I didn't concentrate on the pain, because the feeling of freedom was both intoxicating and worrisome. I felt there was something clean about the forest, clean about the refuge away from the lice and dirt, away from the misery of the men in the camp. Yet fear filled me as I realized I was severely handicapped. There was no doubt that I had injured my hip, but I started walking despite the pain. The night was freezing cold, and I shivered. Luckily there was no wind. I thought of my comrades behind the barbed wire in the camp. They must be dividing the bread now, I

ESCAPE

thought. I felt sure that everyone was talking about my escape.

Despite my freedom, I felt terribly lonely and scared. A thousand thoughts raced through my mind. I lost some of my faith in myself and cursed my bad luck. I blamed myself for indulging in this desperate fantasy. Leave it to me and I'd botch it up sooner or later, as I always had.

I saw myself as a young boy, back from an errand at the grocery store. "Yurek, can't you do anything right?" asked my mother, exasperated. "I sent you for a pound of sugar, and look at you. You lost half of it through a hole in the bag! And the naphtha for the lamp you forgot altogether!"

Yes, I saw myself as a failure and an impractical dreamer. Fantasizing I could do very well, but who needed that? This was reality: the dark forest on a freezing winter night with German patrols hunting for me.

My hip was aflame with pain. I found a sturdy branch and used it as a walking stick. It was a long night. As I made my way through the dark forest I recalled another escape I had made many years before, when I was a child. That time I'd run away from home because I had embarrassed my father with one of my pranks.

RUNAWAY FROM HOME

That incident began quietly. One day, when I was about eight, I sneaked into the garden of our neighbor, Mrs. Bogalski, with my new slingshot and practiced shooting down her tomatoes. I had made the slingshot myself with rubber tubing tied to a Y-shaped maple branch that I'd carefully selected. For ammunition I used some small pebbles that filled the pockets of my shorts.

Perfecting my marksmanship had become an obsession with me. Not only did I like to skip pebbles over the surface of a pond, but I also enjoyed making various targets and then trying to hit them with small rocks. I was getting quite proficient.

As I sat carefully camouflaged in the shadow of some lilac bushes, I proceeded to smash up Mrs. Bogalski's tomatoes. I placed a pebble firmly in the leather patch, stretched the tubing, aimed and let go the pebble. It swished into the target . . . and released a splatter of red. I was so engrossed in my marksmanship that I didn't notice Mrs. Bogalski standing right behind me. She was a large, strong woman. She grabbed me by the back of my shirt collar and dragged me screaming to my father. "Mr. Schoolmaster," she shouted, "teach your own brat first before you teach other children!"

My father was furious. He took hold of my ear and pulled me into a small room. Then he took off his belt, bent me down by my neck over a chair and belted my bare behind. I cried out in pain. "Will you ever do anything like that again?" he barked.

"No! Never! I promise!" I cried. Finally, he stopped. Then he immediately demanded that I kiss his hand and ask his forgiveness. He extended his hand. I couldn't do it. I grabbed my shorts and dashed from the room.

I knew I'd been bad and that what I had done to the tomatoes was wrong. But I felt he didn't have to be so mean. I had made enough noise while he was hitting me to satisfy Mrs. Bogalski, who was waiting within earshot of our house. But I also felt my father wasn't beating me just for her benefit; I felt his rage went beyond this incident, and that he resented me for just being me. That's why I decided to run away, to show him that I didn't need him.

I ran and hid in our garden, a safe distance away. From there I watched him, still shaking with anger, calling me. But I wouldn't go back. I'm not a dog, I told myself. I'm not going to run to him and kiss his hand. I'll show him!

I stayed there a long time. Eventually I saw him get on his bicycle and go off, probably to the post office. Now's my chance, I thought. I ran to the kitchen and cut two slices of bread, spread some butter and cheese on them and wrapped them in a piece of paper. Then I fetched my little violin, a recent birthday present. I don't know why I did that. Probably because it was my most prized possession. But as it turned out, it was fortunate that I took it. I put the food and the violin in a cloth sack and sneaked out of the house.

It was a nice summer day. I'll hide among the trees, I thought. No one will find me there. I looked around and realized that no one had seen me leave. In a little while I reached the edge of the forest.

It was dark and quiet there, like an empty church. I walked deeper into the woods and thought of the mushrooms and berries the village women picked around here. I remembered that, during the summer months, I used to see them coming down the sandy road, carrying their full baskets. They sang as they walked, kicking up clouds of dust with their bare feet. I admired those peasant feet, so strong and calloused, their toes spread wide apart. They looked like they never needed shoes. The women were young and robust, and their sunburned faces glowed. Strands of flaxen hair peeked out from under the colorful kerchiefs that covered their heads, and their full, flowery skirts billowed around their legs. They would often stop at my house to sell their bounty to my mother. So this is where they picked, I thought. Right here!

I looked up and saw the tall masts of fir trees converging into a point above my head. A cuckoo's call echoed strangely and then suddenly stopped as a bolt of lightning tore through the darkening forest. A clap of thunder followed, and soon it started to rain. Quickly I found shelter under some dense foliage and felt a shiver of fear run down my spine. I could go back, I thought, but . . . no! I was still too hurt and angry. I'd stay and suffer whatever might happen.

After a while the rain stopped and night fell. I suddenly remembered my sandwich. I ate it hungrily. Then I lay down and tried to fall asleep. But it was dark and spooky all around, and I heard strange noises. Probably some innocent little rabbits, I tried to reassure myself, but at the same time my imagination suggested something much more dangerous. Could it be a wolf or a bear? Then I thought of my parents. They must be worried by now, I felt, and were probably searching for me. Well, I'd showed them!

The night became colder, and I shivered. I removed the violin from the cloth sack and covered myself with the sack as best I could. Then I dozed off, but only briefly. Strange noises would awaken me. Then I'd doze off again. That became the pattern of the night. Finally, it was morning. I put my violin back in the sack and started walking. Soon I came to a clearing and warmed myself in the sun. There I noticed an abundance of blueberries. Good, I thought, this will be my breakfast. After eating, I fell asleep in the sun, and when I woke up I realized that I had no plan to follow. It started to dawn on me that this escape was just a way to show my father that I could fight back. The whole idea suddenly seemed very silly. I stood up and decided to return home.

I started walking and, after changing direction several times, realized I was lost. I couldn't even find the blueberry patch I had recently plundered. Then I thought: Could it be possible that the village girls were picking berries today? If only I could find them. An idea came to me, and I took out my violin and started to play. As the weird sounds echoed through the forest, two women suddenly appeared among the trees. Naturally, they were very surprised to see me.

"Aren't you the schoolmaster's son?" one of them asked. I was happy they knew me. "I ran away from home," I confessed, "but I think I'd better go back with you."

When I finally got there, my mother was crying and my father looked drained. He didn't even hit me. They were so relieved. They'd been up all night looking for me.

RECAPTURE AND PUNISHMENT

I shivered with cold and realized I was not a little boy anymore. This time my escape was real.

I walked, leaning heavily on my stick and wincing in pain. Could I continue in this condition for 10 days, I wondered. I felt disoriented and my spirits were low. Well, I'll give it my best, I told myself as I limped through the woods.

It was late at night when I came to a clearing near a river. For a while I walked along the river bank, but when I saw the river was going to change course I decided to cross it. It was so narrow at that point I felt I could manage. There were clumps of frozen grass and ice floes that formed a natural path. I was already several steps across when the ice suddenly gave way and I plunged into the frigid water. Gagging, thrashing about and almost drowning, I somehow managed to make it to the other side. I crawled up the river bank and collapsed, limp as a rag. The next thing I remember was seeing the black jackboots of German soldiers towering above me.

Suddenly, it was all over. This was the end. They didn't have to capture me. The didn't have to shoot me. I was theirs. I didn't care what happened to me as I lay there, half dead, at their feet.

They could have shot me on the spot. But I think they realized that if they did, they'd have to carry my body back to camp. Instead, they prodded me with their rifles, got me to my feet and marched me back to camp.

I had previously figured out that the woods I had escaped to were north of the camp, and that Switzerland was to the south. So I'd had to go around the camp. I had walked for hours in as wide an arc as I could, but obviously not wide enough.

At the guardhouse, I was told to take off all my wet clothes, and I stood there, naked and shivering, while the sergeant of the guards sprawled out in his swivel chair and bombarded me with questions. "Who helped you escape?" he demanded. "Was the woman in the house helping you? Answer me! Louder, you damned Polish pig!"

"No, no one helped me," I stuttered in my lame German.

"You liar! Tell the truth!" he screamed and nodded to a guard, who ran over to me and smacked me so hard across my face I thought he had broken my neck. Then, with another blow he knocked me to the floor and viciously kicked me. I saw blood on my belly and realized my nose was bleeding profusely. I moaned, shielding myself from the soldier's wrath. Then the beating was over and, still naked, I was pushed into a cell and left alone.

The solitary confinement cell was an eight-by-four-foot concrete cubicle. There was nothing in it, not even anything to sit on. Desperately, I started to exercise. I moved around, despite the pain, which I felt all over my body. When I couldn't move anymore, I slapped myself wherever I could reach in order to keep from freezing.

It was an incredibly long night, perhaps the longest of my life. Every minute that passed seemed like a painful test of my endurance and a monumental achievement. Every minute was a witness to my survival. The cell was like an upright coffin. It didn't have a window, and there was no way I could tell when the night would be over. I relied on sounds, which increased with the advent of morning.

Finally, the door opened, and someone threw in my half-wet clothes. I was escorted to a latrine and given a cup of ersatz tea. A few minutes after being returned to my cell, the door opened again. A *feldfebel* (guard) came in, screaming at me. He knocked me to the floor and kicked me until I moaned with pain.

For the next two weeks I received a portion of bread and water every second day, and some soup at noontime. I ached all over from the beatings and kickings I received two or three times a day. The *feldfebel's* gold tooth gleamed in his sadistic grin as he assaulted me. I learned how to protect my head and face with my arms and hands. I also learned to exaggerate my expressions of pain, because I knew my cries and moans appeased him. Sometimes he would make me run in circles in the prison yard while firing his revolver toward me and screaming: "*Schnell!* Fast!"

They clipped off all my hair and painted the large, white numerals *11091*, my POW number, on the back of my army coat. After a few days, the beatings diminished, and I realized the mere fact that I was still alive was a miracle. That I was clothed, fed and healing was a luxury.

Eventually I was transferred to a regular cell, which contained a sleeping cot. High above was a dirty little window, too small to even consider in terms of escape.

ESCAPE INTO DANGER

RECAPTURE AND PUNISHMENT

However, the window delighted me, because it was my link to the outside world. Fortunately, it was broken and missing a piece of glass. Through it I could see the sky and the small branch of a tree. I could also hear noises from the outside. I listened, trying to see a picture of my surroundings with my mind's eye. That way I could mentally visualize a lot of the action taking place outside my cell. At times I heard a truck stop at the gatehouse and then the shout of commands to board it. One day, hardly believing my ears, I heard Kazik singing his psuedo-Italian arias! I wondered whether he knew that I was able to hear him.

After a few weeks I was told that I would be transferred to another camp in Germany, near Hagenau. "That camp will teach you not to try to escape anymore," a guard said to me as he pushed me into a waiting truck. On the way, we picked up some other prisoners.

It was March, and the winter frost gave way to a constant rain that penetrated our bodies to the bone with chill. Eventually we were dropped off at a penal camp.

PENAL CAMP

The camp was in a wooded area and had only recently been built. It consisted primarily of a long row of barracks. The security was so strict there was virtually no chance for escape. I saw guards with dogs patrolling all peripheries of the camp.

After passing through the gate, our truck stopped at the yard for roll call. Prompted by the guards shrieking *"Alle raus!* Everyone out!" we scrambled down from the trucks and formed a line to be counted. Then the barracks capos came and assigned us to bunks. As I looked around, I saw many prisoners like myself whose coats were marked with large, white numerals.

My new companions eagerly asked me about my escape and the conditions at Weissenburg. We talked late into the night, and when morning came with the sudden blast of whistles, I followed the others into the yard for roll call. After the head count, we were warned to strictly obey all the camp rules. I noticed an unusually large number of guards with dogs patrolling both inside the camp and outside its borders.

It was a chilly, gray March morning. The sun struggled to emerge from behind the clouds as we walked in small groups toward the river. Our job was to retrieve the barbed wire that was strewn all around. We had to roll it over wooden poles and then carry those heavy, thorny spools to a distant railroad depot.

"Hey, buddy," I said to my partner. "My name's Yurek. What's yours?"

"Thomas," he replied.

"Listen, Thomas," I said, "let's use our brains. These spools are heavy. Let's wind them loosely."

He agreed, and we got away with a couple of lighter trips before a watchful guard noticed our ploy and sicced his German shepherd on us. To the guard's amusement, the dog nipped at our heels, forcing us to move much faster!

The area where we worked was swampland, and the air stank from rotting vegetation, animal carrion and perhaps even the dead bodies of soldiers. It bred billions of tiny black flies, which crawled into our eyes, ears and nostrils, driving us crazy. It was sheer torture. We didn't dare drop our loads to wipe our faces, because if we did, the dogs would be on us immediately. At day's end we not only rested our dead-tired bodies but also nursed our dog bites. The old-timers had learned to protect their legs with scraps of wood or metal. I soon followed their example.

It angered me that our work supplied barbed wire to help the Nazis entrap their enemies. I couldn't come to terms with that, though I knew I couldn't change it. And the Germans knew the value of our work. We even received more food than in the previous camp, probably so that we would last longer and work harder.

Eventually, spring gave way to a hot, sweaty summer, and the curse of the little black flies was finally gone. We cleared all the barbed wire from the area, and the camp closed. Then we were loaded into trucks and sent to a big transit camp in Strassburg, often referred to by prisoners as "the Catacombs" because of its subterranean passages and rooms. The building was part of the city's ancient fortification.

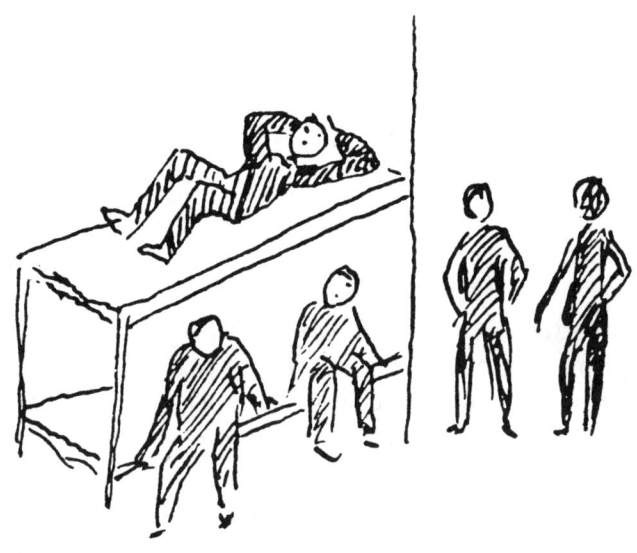

CATACOMBS

The subterranean rooms where we were housed were damp and cold. In many places water trickled down the walls. A maze of two-tier bunkbeds made the dormitory almost impassable. I walked with a capo to my destination. "The top one up there is yours, pal," he said, and I climbed up to check out my straw bag. That's when I saw Sobish. He was sitting on his bunk deep in thought. Delighted, I ran over to him. "Hey, Sobish!" I yelled. "It's half a year since I saw you! God, your beard grew longer." We hugged each other.

"Yurek!" he exclaimed, beaming. "I often wondered what became of you. How've you been? Christ, we have a lot to talk about!" Sobish rarely displayed emotion, but he was clearly thrilled by this unexpected reunion. After the division of bread, we settled down to talk.

"I've got some bad news," he said quietly. "Remember the day Janek was hit between the eyes with a rifle butt? Well, ever since then he wasn't himself. His nose was broken, but that wasn't the worst. He must have suffered some brain damage, because he became disoriented and didn't know where he was. Poor guy. We all felt sorry for him and took care of him as best we could. But we couldn't watch him all the time. Like that last time, when he did a stupid thing." Sobish paused. I wasn't sure he could go on. "The poor sonofabitch got up in the middle of the night and, before anyone noticed, he was at the gate, arguing with the guard, trying to get out. They shot him on the spot."

I shook my head slowly. "Maybe it's better this way," I said sadly. "He probably would have suffered a lot and come to the same end anyway. Obviously he wasn't the same Janek who taught Kazik those Italian arias. Ah, it's too bad." I slapped my forehead with my hand. "Christ, it could have been me!" I muttered.

"No, not you," Sobish said. "You were careful. You knew what would happen if you weren't."

"But," I protested, "look how I botched up my escape because of stupid errors."

"What errors?" he asked. "Tell me about it."

We talked late into the night. By the time we stopped, I saw my escape attempt as a learning experience. The next time I tried it, I promised myself, I'd plan better.

"One has to be very careful," said Sobish. "That's why I'm still here." He sighed, not knowing that later even he could not be careful enough to save his life.

"Well," I agreed, "any time you decide to break out, I'll be glad to keep you company."

"It may be sooner than you think," he said, concluding our talk. "I'll let you in on it when the time comes."

The next day I saw Felek the actor. He was bunked

in the next dormitory. "Hey, Felek," I shouted across the room, "I'm glad you're still kicking around. I thought the guys would have killed you by now for telling all those stories about the food on the cruise ship." We were glad to see each other. I found out that Kazik was still singing arias for the Germans at Weissenburg.

The news trickled into camp about Hitler's invasion of Russia. We also heard that the British had bombed Germany. These were exciting events. Finally, Germany was starting to feel some war damage.

WHERE IS GOD?

Discussions among the men went on late into the night. We touched on many subjects. One's faith and belief in God was a controversial topic. "Religion is the opium of the masses," said Sobish one evening. This statement provoked many responses.

"How can you say that?" someone asked. "My religion helps me live through all this mess. I pray to Jesus, and I know he will save me."

"That's exactly what I mean," Sobish said. "You get so dependent on Jesus and all that stuff, you don't give your brain a chance to figure things out for yourself."

"You mean you don't believe in God?" someone else asked. "Don't you see that life itself is the greatest proof of God's existence?"

WHERE IS GOD?

"Like hell it is!" I jumped in. "If there were a God so mighty, merciful and just, we wouldn't have scum like Hitler and Stalin. No, pal, don't give me that bullshit about God's justice." I was getting worked up. "And let me tell you something else," I continued. "You don't need religion. What you need are brains and heart." They had all become very quiet and were looking at me. "Did you know," I continued, warming to my subject, "that a long time ago people were so primitive they didn't know their assholes from their elbows? Someone had to govern them for their own good. The high priests of Egypt did just that. They were first-class moralists and scientists. They took it upon themselves to rule the masses, often using witchcraft and tricks. For example, take the crocodile, an ugly beast everyone would have liked to kill. Yet that crocodile played a very important role in ancient Egypt. Those reptiles were like the sanitation department. They cleaned the Nile River of all the filth and decay. They fed on it. But try explaining that to the dumb common people. Instead, the high priests proclaimed the beast a god and created a cult of crocodile worshippers. No one was allowed to kill the animal anymore. As a matter of fact," I said, building to my climax, "the stupid idiots even prayed to the damn crocodile. That's what religion is!"

"Exactly," said Sobish and slapped me on the back in agreement.

SINNER

We all turned in. Later that night I woke up and heard heavy snoring all around me. There weren't any windows in that underground dormitory, only one dim, dirty light bulb yielding an uncertain yellow gleam.

I couldn't sleep. I was still angry with the idea of God and sin—yes, above all, with sin. I recalled my early Catholic childhood and the constant fear of punishment for my sins. I remembered especially how the eyes of Holy Mary would follow me wherever I went. Bound in a heavy gold frame, she looked at me from a painting on the living room wall. There was no place to hide from her gaze. I remembered when I was about three years old, sitting on the floor, busily coloring a picture, and when I'd suddenly raise my head there she'd be, looking directly at me. Or if I looked at her as I crossed the room, she would follow me with her sad eyes until I tripped over a chair. And she would continue looking at me with an imperceptible little smile lingering at the corners of her mouth, amused, knowing I could not escape her gaze.

This didn't worry me then. But later, when I was about four and had become a sinner, it was a big problem. And lying only compounded my sin. I had to lie because I had promised my nurse, Bogusia, that I would never tell anyone about our sex games. I didn't like to lie. But Holy Mary seemed to know about me. I tried to avoid her eyes. I'd walk through the living room with my eyes tightly shut, tripping over various objects. Everyone demanded an explanation for my strange behavior. Obviously, I couldn't tell them the truth. So I lied, inventing reasons. "The light hurts my eyes," I'd say, but they'd insist that there was hardly any light in the room. No one seemed to believe me, and from one lie to another I slipped hopelessly into an abyss of sin.

The world I was living in was full of temptations. Yet wherever I turned, I was up against a warning that hell was waiting for me with all its tortures. I'd see myself being slowly broiled in flames, tended by horrible devils armed with sharp pitchforks. Somewhere above the red smoke and the screaming of the tortured sinners, the sky would open and show the accusing finger of God.

As I grew older, I realized that my whole life was permeated by a very strong religious flavor. "Praise the Lord" was a common greeting, to be answered by "Till the end of ages. Amen." In the course of a day I crossed myself countless times, starting with the morning prayer in the classroom, where a figure of Christ hung on a dark wooden cross on the main wall, and continuing on many occasions until after the night prayer. At the crossroads of our village stood a small statue of Holy Mary. I was taught to cross myself at this junction and recite a prayer. Farther on, I would cross myself again when I passed a terribly bony Jesus dying on a cross.

As I got older, I didn't always follow the rules, and I felt my list of sins was constantly growing. Sundays became particularly difficult. Every Sunday we attended Holy Mass at a nearby church. We went through the rituals of kneeling, standing, bending and chest-pounding while asking God's forgiveness. The organ music trailed slowly, and thin female voices wove agonizingly sad and painful songs of Christ's suffering. In my mind's eye, I saw those singers nude as their sweet voices wafted through the air. I delighted in the shameless practice of mentally undressing the women and girls as I looked at them in church. I knew this was a great sin, according to my prayer book. Yet I was helpless. The sinful visions kept coming from all directions, often at the very moment the priest was sermonizing about sinning.

As Easter approached, the air was full of the mournful singing of *Gorzkie Zale* (Bitter Grievings), commemorating Christ's sufferings. We sang, not only in church, but also at school and at the roadside cross with the dying Christ. These were painful dirges, describing all the gory details of tortured death. Blood was oozing through the punctures made by the crown of thorns. Blood dripped and flowed in little rivulets from the nail wounds in the hands and feet. It ran steadily from the pierced heart. "Eat my flesh and drink my blood," the song went, "and if you have faith in me you'll be saved."

I was awestruck by this terrifying magic and by my own vulnerability. Eventually, when I reached a mile-long list of sins, I decided I had nothing to lose anymore and might just as well be as bad as I wanted.

During the religion class in our elementary school, the children were instructed in the rites of confession and holy communion. The two Protestant children were excused from participation. A priest from the town would come to conduct the class. He had a lot to say about the great suffering of Christ. Sometimes I would challenge him, yet he had clever and pat answers for everything. I was convinced that, with all respect to Christ, he hadn't suffered as much as other people I'd heard about. For instance, I told the priest, I felt that the victims of Chinese tortures suffered more, and asked him how he would like to have a rat eat through his body while he was still alive? Or the victims of the Tartars, who were impaled on sharpened logs standing upright at the crossroads of the Ukraine, gradually and slowly slipping down from their own weight? I felt they would have been glad to be finished off in one day as Christ was. But the priest said it was the suffering of the soul that really counted.

I couldn't help feeling that all these very religious people used the good name of Jesus for their own convenience. Thousands had died in his name during the Crusades. I felt sure that, if Jesus knew about that, he would feel very sorry for the whole bloody Christianization business his name had caused.

The priest was very clever and often talked of damnation in hell, where flames and devils devoured condemned sinners. The only salvation was to beg God's mercy and forgiveness and then to confess one's sins in alphabetical order, with the proper enumeration of circumstances pertaining to the transgressions. Finally, one had to promise never to commit those sins again.

By the time I was 11 and preparing for confession, I felt fear and rage mounting within me. Feeling so vulnerable and cornered, I hated priests. They reminded me of death. On one hand, they appeared to be full of love, though I felt it was slimy love. On the other, they were patronizing, cruel and vindictive. As I sat in my bedroom with my book of the Ten Commandments, the thought of telling someone my most private thoughts and sins made me furious! I picked up a chair and smashed it to the floor. One of the legs broke off with a loud crack.

There was a knock at the door. I heard my mother's

voice and, reluctantly, I let her in. She tried to calm me.

"Dear Sonny," she said. "Tell me—what's wrong? Let me help you."

"No, mother, you don't understand," I wailed. "I hate

the priests. I don't want to tell my sins to anybody, and especially not to them."

"But, Sonny," my mother said, trying to be patient and understanding. "You are not a sinner. How could you be? You're only 11. Now, let's just go together through the Ten Commandments."

Before I knew it, I was trapped. And by my own mother! She read each commandment from the book and asked me how many times I had violated it. Had I done so with my thoughts only, or in any other way? It got so bad that I couldn't talk. I just nodded as she kept questioning.

Finally, we came to my worst sins. Did I think unclean thoughts? Did I talk, touch or do it? How often? I was on the verge of tears.

"Well," she demanded. "Did you do it?" She was one of the last people in my life I wanted to tell!

"Leave me alone!" I screamed. "Just leave me alone!"

But she kept at it. "Did you? Did you?"

"Yes! I did!" I blurted out, furious and crying.

"With whom?" The question hung like an unexploded bomb. "With Bogusia! And others!" I shouted, igniting the fuse.

My mother's face turned ashen. She looked at me in a state of shock. "You mean . . . with all the maids?" she asked.

Then she wanted to know everything. "Did you touch them? Did they touch you? You know where I mean. Did you do other things?" she demanded.

"Yes! Yes! Yes!" I screamed, humiliation, rage and tears erupting in me like a volcano.

"It's incredible," she said, shaking her head in disbelief. "Do you realize you could become diseased and die from such things?"

"I don't *care!*"

"Look me in the eye," she said, staring at me. "Do you know that I can read all your thoughts? They are written in your eyes with little red veins. From now on, you must tell me everything!"

My mother! How I hated her then. Yet in spite of what I had just revealed, I knew she still loved me, even though she said I was unclean and wouldn't touch me.

"Please, mother," I begged. "Don't tell father." My father would beat me with his belt if I embarrassed him. Years later I realized the frustration I must have caused him. After all, he was the schoolmaster and a highly respected man in the community. I did not reflect his virtues. On the contrary, I was often the perpetrator of pranks.

I distinctly remember one of those capers. It happened when I was about five. You might ask how I remember my age so well. Well, at five I wore blue velvet knee-pants with a rear flap, which would fall open if the buttons on each side of the waist were undone. My village playmates often teased me because of my fancy clothing. They were poor and barefoot. Their lunch often consisted of two hunks of bread spread with lard and wrapped in newspaper, while I walked around like a little prince in my velvet outfit with its white-embroidered Fauntleroy collar. One day they dared me to stand in the middle of the road with my rear flap open and my bare behind aimed at an approaching automobile. I have to point out that this was not a dangerous enterprise; the road that passed our house was not a main highway, but a secondary dirt road, and the occasional car going by would have been a model-T Ford that moved slowly up the steep hill. But this made no difference to my father, who belted my bare behind in order to teach me respectful behavior worthy of a schoolmaster's son.

As Easter approached, my mother looked at me as if I were a leper. I had difficulty lying to her now that I knew she could read my eyes. But I also felt she had tricked me in order to find out my secrets. It took many years for me to forgive her for her intrusions on my privacy, but eventually I did. After all, I realized, she meant well, and I knew she loved me.

Toward morning, after this long night of memories, I finally fell asleep. I dreamed I was painting my mother's portrait. I painted her eyes in such a way that they always followed me, like the eyes of Holy Mary in the living room when I was little.

POOR SOBISH

Startled, I woke up to the blasts of the morning whistles as another day made its way onto my seemingly endless calendar of POW experiences.

We didn't have any blankets in the Catacombs. At night we took off our pants and shirts, bunched them up to make pillows and covered ourselves with our army coats. No wonder it came to us as a great surprise when one day we were suddenly issued blankets. Why? we wondered. Are they losing the war and trying to be nice to us?

Soon the news filtered through. The International Red Cross Commission from Switzerland had been invited to examine the conditions in the camp. On the day of the visit, a high-ranking Nazi officer checked our dormitory to see that all was in order—blankets neatly covering the straw bags, floors swept clean. Even the soup was thicker.

POOR SOBISH

We watched with interest as several well-dressed civilians, accompanied by German officers, strolled through our dormitory. We were told to stand at attention while the members of the commission stopped here and there to ask questions of the prisoners. When they stopped in front of Sobish, they inquired, "How are the Germans treating you?"

"Excellent," Sobish answered, with obvious sarcasm. "They even gave us blankets for a special occasion like this."

The commission members were puzzled and whispered among themselves as the guards watched. As soon as the inspection was over, the blankets were retrieved and taken back to the warehouse.

That evening a German officer and two guards came into our room. Obviously looking for someone, they soon spotted Sobish because of his beard. The officer pointed to him and the two guards grabbed Sobish. "*Raus!*" screamed the officer, red with anger. They took him to solitary confinement. The next day we learned they had beaten him to death. "Poor Sobish," I grieved. "And he was always so careful."

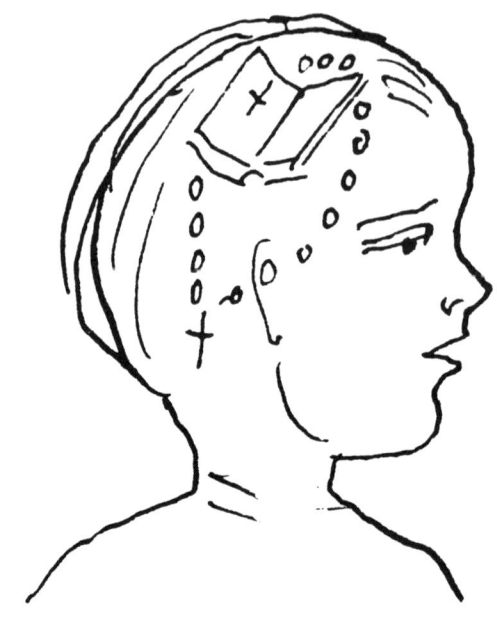

YOUSEK

As evening came, we sorely missed our friend, who only the night before had participated in our discussions. "God must have punished him," said the fellow who occupied the bunk directly under mine. His name was Yousek Podolak, a slight young man in his 20s who displayed so little personality he was barely visible. Yousek was a simple, uneducated fellow whose philosophy of life could be summed up in a few short words: lie low, keep quiet, follow the leader and trust in God. "Why should God punish Sobish?" I asked him.

"Remember last night, when Sobish talked against religion?" he answered. "Well, maybe that's why God punished him."

"But what about me?" I asked, caustically. "Why didn't God punish me? I talked more against Him than Sobish did."

"Well," said Yousek, "you must be one of those lucky guys who always get away with things. Maybe you'll get punished later, in hell."

"The same to you, buddy," I snapped. "What makes you think you're so perfect?"

"Oh, never mind," said Yousek, who couldn't carry the conversation any further. He opened his pocket prayer book and tried to redeem his soul.

Despite the fact that Yousek differed with me on religious matters, he must have thought highly of me in other ways, because a few days later he asked me to let him come along if I should decide to escape. Perhaps he admired me because of my first attempt. At any rate, Yousek was obviously ready to put his fate in my hands. As for me, I wasn't enthralled with the idea of Yousek's company; yet his request bolstered my self-confidence. The fact that Yousek was willing to entrust his life to my leadership meant to me that I must be a more valuable person than I'd given myself credit for. So I began to seriously consider the possibilities of another escape.

PLANNING THE RUSE

It was in the prison yard a few days later that a prisoner who had recently been caught trying to escape was being escorted to detention by a prison guard. As the prisoner passed me, he brushed against me and unobtrusively handed me a small compass. Perhaps he felt it was too dangerous to keep on his person. But that chance encounter would change my life. The little compass would, a short time later, lead me out of prison and away from the Nazis.

Frankly, I didn't think very much of my escape capabilities. After being caught and paying so dearly for it, I was inclined to be very cautious about any new opportunities that might present themselves. I'd also lost some of my spirit and faith in myself. On the other hand, I was flattered that Yousek had asked to come with me. It was such a declaration of confidence in me, since I was only 18 then

PLANNING THE RUSE

and a few years younger than he. Even though his request came from a man frequently dependent on others, his faith in me helped me feel more capable. I felt that maybe I *could* do it, after all. So I told Yousek I'd take him with me, but I added: "You will have to do exactly as I say."

One night toward mid-October 1941, we heard the steady drone of British bombers in the distance, followed by a series of explosions. It must be Karlsruhe getting hit, I thought. That town was nearby. Good, now the Nazis are getting a taste of their own medicine, I thought. During the next few days, the guards started selecting prisoners for work details outside the camp. We speculated that the Germans needed us to dig air-raid shelters. Several work groups were formed before I was finally chosen to be in one. Miraculously, Yousek was also put in my group.

Early the next morning we were herded into two trucks and, about an hour later, arrived at a small village. There we were subdivided into smaller groups of 12 and had only two guards watching us. This looks promising, I thought to myself. A new work group. A new place. No one's tried anything here yet, so security will probably be more relaxed.

Shovels and spades were distributed, and we started digging ditches. The weather was very pleasant, and it was good to be away from the dingy Catacombs. I was happy to feast my eyes on the green gardens and vineyards.

Without wasting any time, I began plotting my second escape. When I'd conceived a plan, I let Yousek know, in a low whisper, that I expected to break out in a few days. Yes, he said, he'd be ready. That night I briefed him. I felt responsible for him and was trying to do my best this time.

Unfortunately, the woods were quite a distance away from where we dug, so we'd have to hide somewhere in the immediate area first, perhaps in the vineyards, which were numerous. The village itself was surrounded by flat brown stretches of freshly plowed fields. Even a

ESCAPE INTO DANGER

rabbit couldn't get out of here without being seen, I thought. So it will have to be the vineyards first. I also knew that timing would be very important. At the end of the day, around five o'clock, while we were cleaning our shovels, would be best, and we'd have to hope that dusk would come quickly. If they searched the vineyards—the obvious hiding place—they'd find us easily if it were still light. I also realized that, before they were free to search for us, they'd have to load all the other prisoners on the trucks and guard them. So I knew I'd have to figure out some kind of ruse.

The plan came to me while we were digging. Nearby was a farm building obviously used for storage. It was surrounded by several bushes. At ground level I noticed some dusty metal slides protruding from the cellar windows, probably used for sliding down sacks of grain to be stored. I'll make them think we're in the cellar or some other part of the building, I thought. That'll be the ruse. I'll ask a guard to let me urinate in the bushes. Then I'll wrap my jacket around my shovel and reach down the slide as far as I can, wiping the dust away. It'll look as if someone had just slid down. While they search the building, they'll lose precious time before dusk. Only then would they start to search the vineyards. At the same time, they'll still have to guard the rest of the prisoners, who, seizing the opportunity, might also try to escape. Hopefully, it'd be too late to call for extra guards with dogs. I was terrified of dogs. They could sniff us out in no time. So, I thought, that will be it.

Over the next few days, Yousek and I saved some of our bread rations, figuring that, once we got away, we'd find some vegetables and berries in the fields. And so, one crisp October morning—October 25, to be exact—we were ready. Again, the fear of this undertaking made me ill and nauseous. I imagined myself being shot by the guards. Then, realizing how negative those thoughts were, I concentrated on seeing myself free and the escape a *fait accompli*. Though that made me feel better, I was still very nervous as I watched the time creeping closer.

To get the guards used to the idea of our urinating in the bushes, we repeated this maneuver several times. As planned, I wiped the thick dust off a metal slide, an obvious sign of entry into the cellar, and then returned to dig in the trenches.

Finally, five o'clock neared. The guards were busy talking and flirting with some peasant girls who had come by carrying baskets of grapes. We were cleaning our shovels. I signaled Yousek and slipped out toward the bushes, hoping he would follow. He did.

RUN FOR YOUR LIFE

Suddenly, we were totally committed. Like two arrows released from a bowstring, we knew only one direction. There was no way back to the comparative safety of the prison camp. This was the most important moment in our gamble for freedom, a moment that seemed to last forever, filled with fear, commitment and frantic, yet premeditated, action.

We ran for our lives, crouching low, scrambling on our knees and elbows, taking cover behind the bushes. Then we ran for the vineyard, where green corridors soon closed in around us. Frantically we crawled deeper and deeper into the vineyard. There we lay on our backs under the wire supports and covered ourselves with large green leaves, holding our breath, staying deathly still.

RUN FOR YOUR LIFE

I heard my heart pounding so hard I was terrified it could be heard back at the trenches and betray us. As the churchbells tolled five o'clock, rifle shots rang out. They knew we were gone. We heard frantic shouts, then the shrieks of commands, then the thumping of heavy boots. They could be here soon, I thought. But no. I heard them far away, probably searching the cellar, shouting at prisoners and yelling to each other. We held our breath, camouflaged by the leaves. After a few moments passed, I felt sure they had bitten our bait. Through an opening in the leaves I watched a red apple at the top of a tree catch the last rays of sunlight.

Flies buzzed in my ear, and ants crawled over my face. But I dared not move.

What seemed an eternity went by. Then the clock in the church tower chimed six times. I heard a horse-drawn cart slowly rattle down the road, and the chatter of children's voices. Suddenly there was a loud shout close to where I lay, and I held my breath as I saw a long coat swish by. The heavy boots of the German guard were within my arm's reach. "Not here," he shouted as he turned away, plucking a bunch of grapes.

It was getting dark now. The voices subsided. Soon we heard the trucks starting up and leaving for camp . . . without us.

I didn't dare let my emotions erupt. Not yet. We stayed put till it was very dark, and only then did we slowly, inch by inch, get to our feet.

I took a deep breath and exulted in everything around me. We looked at each other but didn't speak. I ached all over. Then, very slowly and carefully, we started to walk. But as soon as we came out of the vineyard, we found ourselves stepping on some large cabbage heads. The loud squeaks broke the night's stillness, and we froze with fear. The night was like black velvet, and the tolling of church bells resonated from village to village over the

ESCAPE INTO DANGER

silence. Freedom choked our throats; we were awed by the incredulity of our success. Above and far away, the friendly stars of Orion beckoned, pointing the way. I set my little compass. Briskly, we started walking toward Switzerland.

STEALTHY HIKE

We walked very fast, relying on my phosphorescent compass. The night was chilly and silent. The endless flat fields smelled of freshly plowed earth. Hours passed. Finally, we stopped to rest. We lay on a mound of potato weeds and were just starting to doze off when we were startled by a large bird that suddenly swooped down on us and, just as quickly, flew off silently into the darkness. This prompted us to get moving, and we started walking again, skirting the farms and listening carefully for any signs of danger. As dawn diluted the darkness, a little town appeared ahead, nestled between the hillfolds of the Alsatian landscape.

"We'll have to find a hideout pretty soon," I told Yousek, "so we can keep out of sight during the day." Shortly after, we came upon a clump of trees fringed by

STEALTHY HIKE

dense bushes. Very carefully we camouflaged ourselves and, exhausted, fell sound asleep. Suddenly we were abruptly awakened by the sounds of someone crunching through the underbrush. With our hearts in our throats we listened, frozen, not daring to move, searching only with our eyes. But it was only some children running through the woods.

We ate part of our bread rations and rested, waiting for the long hours to pass and bring the cover of night. As dusk approached, we slowly moved to the edge of the wood and surveyed our future path.

The air was still and cold. I could smell the smoke rising from the chimneys of houses nearby. With my mind's eye, I could see families sitting around their kitchen tables. So close was a normal world with people who were free! I *longed* for that kind of life. And then I thought: *We're on our way to getting it.*

MIDNIGHT BLUFF

The town was very small. To circumvent it would mean a difficult trek through hills. All things considered, I decided it would be best to take our chances and just walk right through it. The idea was daring, but the more I thought about it, the better it seemed. The night was dark and, as an air-raid precaution, no lights were allowed. We could be out of there in a few minutes. All we had to do was walk briskly and not arouse suspicion. In the darkness everyone looked the same. I told Yousek of my plan and, as usual, he agreed with me. I found some wet soil and muddied the white numerals on the back of my coat.

By now it was completely dark. We sneaked out of the woods and started walking on the main road. A few people passed, making their presence known only by the sound of their boots. Someone's flashlight skirted over our feet. Another yelled out, *"Verdunkelung!"* warning of the blackout, and the light was instantly extinguished. Within minutes, we were out of the town. Our bluff had worked!

I consulted my compass, and we turned into some wooded hills. According to my calculations, it would take us about 10 days to reach Switzerland. As soon as we could get out of these woods and into some farm fields, we should be able to find some vegetables, I thought. It was the end of October, and I felt we'd have a chance of finding some sugar beets, cauliflower or turnips. We walked all night through the difficult, hilly terrain.

CORNERED

It was dawn when we saw a little village up ahead. By then we were out of the hills and crossing some open fields. The morning sun had just started to break through, and we frantically looked for a suitable hiding place. A clump of dense bushes in the open fields would have to do, I thought. There was no other choice. We burrowed among the leaves and branches and, after a while, fell asleep.

Suddenly I awoke to the sound of a human voice. I peered through the foliage and saw a farmer talking to his horse. He was plowing a field nearby, getting closer to us with each round. This was an untenable situation. There wasn't enough room to hide, and the farmer was bound to discover us after a few more turns. Yousek was trembling with fear, his lips mumbling prayers. There was no time to lose. During the next round, as soon as the farmer turned his back on us, we ran for a deep ditch several hundred yards away on the other side of the road. How stupid of me, I berated myself right afterward! Surely the farmer will notice our tracks on the freshly plowed soil. But by then it was too late.

As we hid in the ditch, however, it occurred to me there was a good chance the farmer could be French, not German. There were many French living in that area. Like a swarm of angry bees, these thoughts buzzed around in my head.

Fortunately, the ditch was deep enough to hide us. From time to time an automobile or horse cart went by only a few feet away, but we weren't visible. Hours passed while we were pinned in that dangerous situation.

Then, suddenly, we heard some stirring nearby, and a small shadow darkened one side of the ditch. From above, a young girl of about nine or 10 looked down at us. Our terror changed to joy as the child smiled, clutching to her chest a loaf of fresh bread and half a bottle of wine. Without a word, she handed these to me and quickly vanished beyond the edge.

Again luck was with us. The farmer was obviously French, after all, and must have realized who we were. The bread and wine he sent us made a great feast. Then we waited for dusk. It was dark when we abandoned our hideout and set out to the south.

NIGHT HUNTER

We walked most of the night. By dawn we had found a convenient shelter in the dense shrubs of some willows. We slept, alternating the time of watch. Finally, the daylight dissipated, and again dusk enveloped us in its protective darkness. But not for long. A bright moon crawled out from behind the clouds.

We stirred and rose. Then, before taking the next step, we froze, motionless. On the other side of the bush a hunter was approaching, his shotgun aimed in our direction. We saw him distinctly, yet realized he didn't see us. He had only heard our movement and maybe taken us for some small game. Indeed, the willow leaves and branches played a camouflage game of light and shadow on our faces. We stood petrified, holding our breath, not daring even to blink our eyes, looking straight into the double barrel of his shotgun. Seconds passed like hours. Eventually, the hunter strolled off, leaving us with madly beating hearts.

Again, we were incredibly lucky that he was without a dog. And what if he'd had a dog? I thought. I knew I would have tried to trick him in some way or overpower him. My freedom was too precious to me to give up now. I wouldn't be caught again!

The night was long as we hiked through the woods of Alsace near Colmar. Coming out of them, we encountered swamps. At times we waded up to our knees through the cold, muddy water, pushing our way past swamp rushes and high swaying grasses. Sometimes water birds tore out from under our feet, filling the quiet night with petrifying shrieks. At dawn we slept again, camouflaged in the dense woods.

POSSE

The next day our luck ran out. A farmer riding a horse cart spotted us. He suddenly came out from behind a bend in the dirt road before we had a chance to hide. We kept walking, but I was uneasy. I expected some serious consequences, and I was right. A few hours later we were startled by the baying of dogs, and I realized we were the target of a manhunt. The sounds of the posse grew closer as we ran for our lives through the woods. So that's how it feels, I thought, to be hunted like a rabbit. The dogs were on our scent, and it would only be a matter of time before we were caught. Their baying echoing through the woods made me shiver with fear. Even today, knowing I was the object of that search makes me wake up some nights in a cold sweat.

As we ran in panic, I suddenly noticed a stream.

POSSE

This is a blessing, I thought, as we splashed in and continued running in the shallow water for about a quarter of a mile. Then we ducked into the woods again, hoping the dogs would lose our scent in the water. Indeed, this worked very well. Shortly after, we came upon another stream, which we used in a similar manner—just in case. As darkness fell, we knew we had outwitted the posse and the dogs. That night we forced ourselves to cover a longer stretch than usual, to outdistance the danger even further. Even after dawn we continued to hike through the woods, taking advantage of the protective trees and bushes. At some point I realized we had walked for two whole nights and days without a respite. Finally, totally exhausted, we camouflaged ourselves in some dense bush and slept, alternating lookout watch.

The nights were getting colder, and we experienced our first frost, which continued through the following nights. I assumed we now were close to the Swiss border, and hiking became more dangerous.

Having eaten our supply of bread, we now ate sweet sugar beets that we found in the fields. At one point we were terribly thirsty, and I daydreamed of a bunch of cold, juicy grapes. That night, groping blindly through the bushes in complete darkness, I felt wires. As I was squeezing through this obstacle, something cold and wet touched my face. Incredulous and disbelieving, I suddenly realized that we were in a vineyard, and that cool, juicy grapes were all around us. There is someone out there, I thought, guiding me, and I felt very strongly it must be my mother's love.

DEAD MAN'S SHOES

Walking was very difficult for me by then because my shoes had cut deeply into the heels of my feet. The shoes that had been given to us in POW camp came from German soldiers killed on the Russian front. Evidently there had been difficulty removing these jackboots from stiff, dead legs, so the boots had simply been cut below the ankle and slipped off. Later, some felt fabric was sewn on for the upper part, and such shoes were distributed to the POW prisoners who worked in the out-of-camp details. There was a sharp ridge where the leather and felt were joined, and this ridge caused cuts and blisters. When it cut deeply into my heels, every step was torture. I tore off a piece of fabric from my shirt, bandaged my feet and kept on walking, wincing and cursing in pain. Yousek followed my example. He and I rarely talked to each other, only communicating the dangers ahead and planning what to do next.

THE LONGEST DAY

It was still dark, just before daybreak, when we came upon a canal near the town of Mulhouse. We had to cross it if we wanted to continue on our Switzerland course. Then we noticed a bridge that was guarded by a German sentry. Very quietly we moved along the canal until we were out of the guard's sight. We stripped and, holding the bundle of our clothes above our heads, swam across. Alas, our clothes got soaked anyway. It was a very cold morning, and everything was covered with a gray frost. The water was shockingly cold—our bodies steamed when we emerged from it. In that dawn light, Yousek looked purple, and, probably, so did I.

Naked and shivering, we wrung out our clothes and put them on, but no sooner were we dressed than we heard sharp German commands a short distance away. We buried ourselves in the underbrush and fallen leaves. Shaking with fear, we observed our new environment.

After a few moments we realized we were hiding on a firing range, and that we were very close to the targets that had been backed against the canal. From all around us came the sharp reports of firearms. We knew we were grounded and must remain there, motionless, until dusk. It was one of the longest days of my life: I lay there, not daring to move for fear of being detected, the wet clothes clinging to me, sending cold shivers all over my body. At times I was afraid that the chattering of my teeth was loud enough to betray our presence. The fear and the cold on an empty stomach were almost too much to bear. We counted the long minutes and hours until darkness. Finally, the soldiers left and night fell. Slowly, we got up. I felt dizzy and weak. It seemed the whole world was spinning before me, and I fell. The idea of being ill and incapacitated both frightened me and made me terribly angry. With all the willpower I could summon, I got up, and, like a drunken man, I lurched along. Yousek was in better shape. I soon realized that I was at the end of my physical strength, and we sat down to talk.

EDGE OF ENDURANCE

"We must find shelter tonight," I told Yousek. "I don't think I can go on much longer. I feel sick." I told him a plan I had been considering. "Let's continue along this road," I said, "and if we see a farmhouse, I'll speak French and ask for shelter for the night. If they answer in German, I'll ask in German for directions to the township house. In the dark they will hardly see us, and I think we could pass for itinerant field workers." Yousek, as always, agreed with me, and we walked down the country road.

When we saw lights from an approaching automobile, we ducked into a ditch. We covered a considerable distance this way and eventually came upon a farm. Dogs started barking, and soon we heard some coarse scolding words in German. "*Wer da?*" a man yelled out in the dark.

Quickly I answered, in German, "We're looking for

the township house to report to." I was delighted to learn that it was only a short distance ahead. I thanked him, and seconds later we vanished into the protective night. "Wow," I said to Yousek, "that was a close call! I give myself an A for bluffing!"

Again, we continued walking down the road. Suddenly, from out of nowhere, a teen-age boy on a bicycle appeared. "Hey, *didonc!*" I called out in French. "Hey, you!"

The youth stopped and responded in that language.

"Are you French?" I asked.

"Sure," he replied. Very quickly and in my best French, I explained our situation. Then I asked him to direct us to a French family who could shelter us for the night. He gave us the information and then vanished into the darkness.

SHELTER WITH LOVE

In a short time we came to the house he told us about, and I knocked on the door. A middle-aged woman opened it, staring at us suspiciously. "Quickly," I said. "Please let us in. We are running from the Germans." For a moment she looked us over. Then she beckoned us in and promptly slammed the door. My God, I thought, I can't believe it! After so many days in the woods, we're finally under a friendly roof. As I glanced down the long entrance hall, I saw something moving. I was ready to bust out and run when I realized I was looking at myself in a full-length mirror! What a horror of a picture I was. My clothes were mangled, torn and covered with mud. My face was dirty, with bloody scratches and bristling with stubble. From dark hollows, my eyes glared with fear and amazement. When I finally turned those eyes away, I saw that my crooked, muddy shoes had left dirty tracks on the shiny wooden floor.

The woman hurried us into the kitchen, where her sister sat. They helped us remove our shoes and coats, and quickly washed the muddy tracks from the floor. Then they heated water, filled a white enamel basin and washed our bleeding feet. Looking at our wounds, they sighed with pity. They bandaged our feet and grieved over us. We talked in a mixture of French and German—being Alsatian, they spoke both.

I found out they were patriotic French. Their brother Andre would be home soon. He worked nearby as a bank clerk. The sisters washed our clothes while we bathed. They gave us clean shirts and pants and then started preparing dinner. In the meantime, I delighted in being clean and warm. I could hardly believe this was actually happening to us.

Soon Andre arrived home on his bicycle and, after being informed of our situation, engaged in a serious talk with his sisters. I understood that we had to be very quiet and not show ourselves at the windows. We were to sleep upstairs and should not put on any lights there. Many German farmers lived in the village, as well as some German soldiers who were guarding a detail of POW field workers. That settled, we proceeded to get acquainted, using French, German and pantomime. They opened a bottle of Calvados, probably saved for a special occasion.

I shall never forget those two brave sisters, Marie and Renee, and their brother, Andre. I knew they had put their lives in jeopardy by giving us shelter. We raised our glasses in a solemn toast. *"Vive la France et Pologne. Mort pour les Boche!"* exclaimed Marie with a sudden fire in her eyes. She reached for a photo album from a nearby shelf. "This is my husband," she said, pointing. "He was killed by the Nazis about a year and a half ago." A tear, like a single pearl, rolled down her cheek and splattered on the photograph of a handsome young man with an elegant black mustache. I stood up and kissed her hand. "I understand," I said softly. "I'm very sorry." Renee, slim and middle-aged, with a sensitive, merciful face, had never married. Neither had Andre, who, like myself, had also been captured in 1940 during the fall of France. Fortunately, he had been released because he lived in Alsace, which was claimed by the Germans as their territory.

Eventually we sat down to dinner, which consisted of hot vegetables and a roasted rabbit. Incredibly, despite my hunger, I couldn't eat much. Then we talked about our plans. After a while, noticing that Yousek and I could hardly keep our heads up, Andre showed us to our beds in the attic.

I fell asleep quickly, but I woke up later that night and had to pinch myself to realize that this wasn't a dream. This was reality, and I was sleeping on clean linens in a real bed away from Germans. Above all, I was free.

Morning came, and again I could hardly believe the luxury of that home shelter. With nervous curiosity I peeked through the curtains and saw a gray morning. The dirty brown street was being pummeled by a fusillade of raindrops. At the end of the block, in front of some houses, I saw a few German soldiers standing, their wet helmets gleaming dangerously in the rain. Quickly, I backed away from the window.

Downstairs, Marie and Renee were already busy preparing breakfast. "Did you sleep well?" they wanted to know when we entered the kitchen.

"It was the best sleep I've had in a very long time," I said. Then, looking at the eggs, muffins and jam, I added, "It's been almost two years since I saw an egg." Yousek agreed, nodding. After breakfast, the sisters showed us a place to hide behind the pantry in case of an emergency.

The house was cozy and pleasant, decorated in an old-fashioned way with lacy curtains and overstuffed furniture. Everything there gave me the feeling of years of family closeness. It reminded me of my home in Poland. A big German shepherd, Morris, trotted in and touched my hand with his cold nose. "He hates Germans," Renee said. She opened the photo album again, and we became acquainted with all their relatives. Outside, the rain continued. It splashed through the ill-fitting rain gutters and soaked the dark, denuded, leafless trees. I thought of how sick I'd felt the day before, how I hadn't thought I could go on, and I was amazed at how quickly I had recovered my strength. I felt that this family's warm acceptance of us—total strangers—was responsible for my quick recovery. That evening Andre returned from work dripping wet, and, as we ate supper, we talked of our plans to cross the border into Switzerland.

"You must let us know that you made it," they said. "Write to us." I took their names, but instead of writing them down, I committed them to memory: *Bourchy Familie, Rue Principal, Habsheim, Alsace*. "You must include the word *Deutschland*," instructed Andre, "because otherwise they will ignore your letter and won't deliver it."

"And, please," interjected Marie, ever cautious, "sign it 'Georgette.'"

Finally, after dinner, night closed in, and it was time to leave. They embraced us and, with tears in their eyes, wished us luck. We thanked them and bade them goodbye. Although the rain had let up, the sisters insisted we each take a black oilcloth poncho. They also prepared some sandwiches for us.

In retrospect, I realize that we never should have taken anything from them, because if we had been caught, we surely would have been tortured to reveal the complicity of this wonderful French family. Quietly, we slipped out the back door and immediately became engulfed in the dark, wet chilly November night. A moment later we were on our way.

LAST STRETCH

Andre led us through the darkness to the road leading to Basel. He rode his bicycle ahead of us, and if he saw anyone approaching he would alert us by turning his head back and whistling. When that happened, we'd hide in a ditch.

We traveled that way for almost an hour. Eventually it came time to part. Again he embraced us. "*Vive la liberte, et bon chance,*" he said, and turned back for home.

We were alone again, but we knew what to expect. There would be barbed-wire fences and guards patrolling the border. We walked very carefully, and, as Andre had directed, we soon left the road and found ourselves in the woods.

"Let's stop and eat," I said. "It's better to carry the food in our stomachs than dangling in our pockets." We sat down on a patch of grass; thinking of our hosts' generosity, we ate all the bread and cheese they had so lovingly prepared for us. "Hey, Yousek," I said cheerfully, "just imagine! Our next meal will be in Switzerland!" It didn't seem possible that we were reaching the finish line of our escape.

Soon after resuming walking, we discovered a barbed-wire fence, and we examined it carefully. It would be foolish to be careless now. It was difficult in the darkness to determine if the fence was electrified, but since I saw no insulators on the wooden posts, I decided it was probably safe. Crawling carefully, we squeezed under, helping each other. Then we stood up and walked toward an opening in the woods. Just ahead must be Switzerland! With that thought, we suddenly heard someone approaching. We lay down, holding our breath. Nearby a German sentry passed, softly humming a tune. The path he was on curved around the woods.

THE FINISH LINE

We lay still, observing the guard's movements. Realizing that daybreak was near, we decided to camouflage ourselves and stay put until night. In the meantime, we studied the pattern in which several guards patrolled the border. As the sky grew pale and dawn uncovered the view in front of us, we saw a freshly plowed field beyond which, clearly visible, stood a border checkpoint on the road we had left just a short while before. A burning question had presented itself to us: Was this checkpoint on the German or Swiss side? We watched a long time for a guard to show himself against the whitewashed booth. When he finally did, we were relieved to see that the uniform he wore was not German. He was Swiss, and beyond him lay our dream. Freedom! My heart was pounding with excitement.

I realized then, at that crucial moment, if anything should go wrong, I would not let myself be taken alive by the Germans. I was prepared to fight like a wildcat. For me it was, more than ever . . . freedom or death!

Praying to unknown gods to protect us from dogs, we lay there completely covered by fallen leaves, only our spying eyes showing. It had stopped raining. As the day passed, we observed and learned. On only one occasion did we have a close encounter—when a passing sentry walked a few feet into the woods to urinate. For a moment he was dangerously close to us. Even after he left, time moved slowly, snail-like, as we lay and waited, constantly measuring with our eyes the distance separating us from freedom.

I tried to count the days since October 25, when we had broken out. Each one seemed filled with action, danger and emergency situations. The constant tension and physical strain made every minute an eternity. It felt as if we had been on the run forever. Yet, according to my calculations, only nine days had passed. It was now November 3.

The hours inched by slowly while we waited for darkness. Finally, twilight gave way to the night. The chill made us shudder and the air carried the scent of decaying leaves and freshly plowed soil. The unmistakable odors of autumn wafted through the low-hanging patches of mist. When it was dark enough, I said to Yousek: "This is the finish line. Keep your eyes open, and when I give you the signal, follow me."

Finally the German guard appeared, and as soon as he passed us, we counted to 25, as rehearsed. "This is it!" I whispered, and we crawled on our elbows and knees. We had only 30 seconds to get out of the sentry's sight. We moved swiftly. The soil felt soft and smelled good. It was quiet, and an ominous stillness filled the night with danger and suspense. I wished it were darker, much darker. I

THE FINISH LINE

crouched low, fearing the deadly crackle of firearms. According to our calculations, the guard was just about to turn around. He couldn't see us yet, though. I hoped he wouldn't turn too soon. Later, at dawn, he'd notice fresh tracks on the soil, but by then it would be too late. We broke out in a run. Another hundred yards separated us from freedom.

OH, GOD, WE DID IT!

We skirted the Swiss guard's booth. Through the lighted window, we could see him reading a newspaper. He was so absorbed he never even looked up. Finally, another hundred yards and we'd be in neutral Switzerland! As the meaning of our success filtered into my awareness, I began to weep. Waves of emotion swept through my body. "Oh, my God," I cried. "We did it! We did it!" Yousek and I fell into each other's arms. Then, after calming down, we walked deeper into Switzerland.

I was puzzled at seeing another sentry booth ahead of us. What's going on? I wondered. Then I recalled studying a map of Switzerland long ago in geography class and remembered how the border in this area wove in and out. Soon after, we saw a road sign, but it was too dark to decipher what it said. I could barely make out that the message was grouped in three sections, one above the other. After thinking about it for a moment, I came to the conclusion that the sign must be a warning against trespassing, worded in the three languages indigenous to Switzerland. "I know we *were* in Switzerland," I told myself. "But wouldn't it be a hell of a joke if we came back into Germany!" With that, and not wanting to push our luck any further, we decided to settle for the rest of the night under cover of our oilskin capes, and we dozed off.

We slept longer than we had intended, for when we woke up to the barking of a dog nearby, the sun was behind us, having just broken through the German horizon to the east. The darkness gave way to a gray morning. The dog, a German shepherd, kept barking as I peeked through an opening in the cape, which covered us like an umbrella. Near the dog I saw a man in a strange military uniform, a feather protruding from his Robin Hood-like hat. He aimed his rifle at us and yelled, "*En avant!* Move forward!" while motioning with his rifle to get up. At his command, the dog stopped barking. As we rose, I hurried to explain that we were POWs running from the Nazis. The Swiss guard was not very communicative. We walked with him to the sentry booth. After consulting with someone on the telephone, he marched us to a road leading to Basel. Yousek was alarmed. "What will happen to us now?" he whispered to me. "Don't worry," I reassured him. "We're in good hands. They have to keep us."

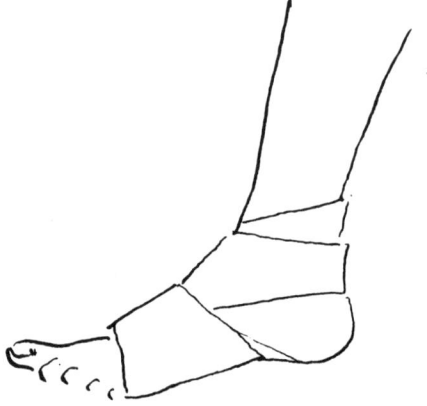

LICKING OUR WOUNDS

Soon the guard, Yousek and I reached the outskirts of Basel, where we boarded a trolley car into town. People smiled at us, and we drank in the feeling of normal life around us.

Finally, the trolley stopped at a large gray building with a sign indicating it was a prison. Here we were given coffee and pastry. We emptied our pockets to produce proof of our identity. The only personal possessions I had were some family photos and some letters. In spite of all that I had been through, I had managed to hold on to these precious items. The inspectors also checked my I.D. tag with my POW #11091. Then we were officially informed that, according to international regulations, we were to be detained in the internment camp *for the duration of the war!* "Well," I thought, "I'll deal with *that* when the time comes." There was no way I was going to sit out the conflict. In the meantime, we were taken to the medical ward, where our feet were properly bandaged. We were given haircuts, food and cigarettes. Then, after bathing, we were permitted to sleep for 24 hours.

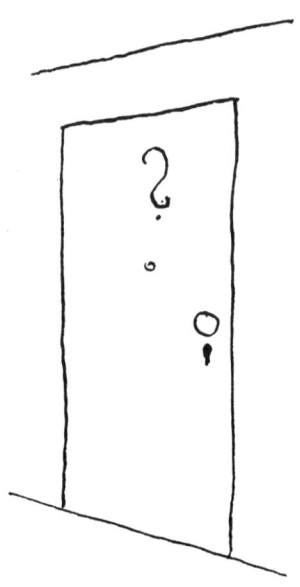

SECRET CONNECTION

Being in prison in Basel did not make me feel like a criminal. I understood that it was a necessary procedure. It was November 1941. I was 19. Instead of staying in an internment camp till the end of the war, I wanted to rejoin the Allied Forces and fight the Nazis. As if by the touch of a magic wand, such an opportunity soon presented itself.

One day we were marched under guard to the railroad station and given two comfortable seats in an elegant compartment on a train headed for Geneva. I had no idea where we were being taken or why. The train stopped at several stations; at the last one a man in a railroad uniform ordered us to exit the train and marched us through the town to an inconspicuous building. There, after we climbed numerous stairs, he knocked in a particular way on a shabby door, its paint peeling.

SECRET CONNECTION

This must be a code, I thought, a sinister feeling of distrust and suspicion growing inside me. The door opened a crack but was blocked by a chain. A moment later we were admitted into a darkened corridor.

Finally another door opened and we entered a brightly lit room. I hadn't yet realized that we were in an office of British Intelligence. In a few minutes, however, I saw clearly that what was wanted from us was information on German troops. We communicated in French, German and sign language. Unfortunately, no one spoke Polish. I had to give them all kinds of detailed information, like describing the insignia on the German uniforms I had seen and where we had dug air-raid shelters. After our British interrogators finished with us, they offered us a cup of tea and biscuits. Then they asked me what I wanted to do. Would I like to be interned in a camp in Switzerland till the end of the war, or would I like to be smuggled into France in order to rejoin the Allied Forces at Gibraltar.

Naturally, I didn't want to stay in Switzerland. With Yousek in agreement, I opted for the latter and put our fate in their hands. They made the necessary arrangements. Once back on the train, we enjoyed the magnificent view of the mountains. Then we dozed off, and when we arrived at Geneva, our ride ended.

A car met us, and we were driven out of town. There, amid the farm fields, stood an old, rust-colored barn. It was getting dark, and a chilly November wind blew over the empty fields. We met other men who were waiting to be smuggled into free France. As night fell, we were told to be very quiet, because the Germans patrolled that area.

Later under cover of darkness, a guide walked us over the border into France and handed our credentials to a Frenchman who suddenly emerged from the shadows. We walked to the small town of Anamase, where we were given a ration of bread; then we boarded a train for Auch. We were told to get off there and someone would meet us.

ESCAPE INTO DANGER

This was a covert operation run by the French Underground: helping escapees from POW camps obtain false documents and getting them to Gibraltar.

INTO FRANCE

As the night train sped in the direction of Auch, I stood in the corridor looking out the window, my forearms on the sill, relishing the ever-growing distance between me and Germany. Presently someone behind me greeted me in the Polish language. *"Dobry wieczor,"* I heard him say. I turned around and saw a well-dressed, middle-aged man looking at me and smiling.

"Good evening," I replied in Polish. "I don't remember you. Have we met before?"

"No," he replied. "I was looking at the bracelet on your wrist, and I thought I saw a Polish name engraved on it."

"You're right," I said. "It is my name. My friend, who was a jeweler, made it for me. It has 12 links made from spoons, and each link has a letter of my name engraved on it. It spells 'Iwaszkiewicz'."

"I thought so," said the stranger. "Is your first name Jerzy?"

"Yes!" I exclaimed. "But how did you know?"

"Frankly speaking, I guessed. But, tell me," he asked quietly, "did you ever know anyone in France who has the same full name as yours?"

"Yes, of course. Captain Jerzy Iwaszkiewicz," I said. "He's my cousin. He was with the Foreign Legion in North Africa. Then he took over the command of a machine-gun outfit on the Maginot Line. But I heard he was killed in action."

"No," said the man. "Your cousin is very much alive and in Marseille. I'll give you his phone number." He reached into his pocket and took out a box of matches. He dumped the match sticks into my hands and wrote a telephone number on the bottom of the inside of the box. Then he replaced the matches and handed the box to me.

"You'd better get off at Lyon and catch a train for Marseille," my new acquaintance said. "Oh, one more thing. Forget you ever met me." He added, barely audibly, "By the way, that phone number lacks the last digit. It's 'one.' You'll have to memorize that."

With that he was gone. I found out later that he was a courier for French Underground operations. He knew my cousin personally, and he'd heard of me.

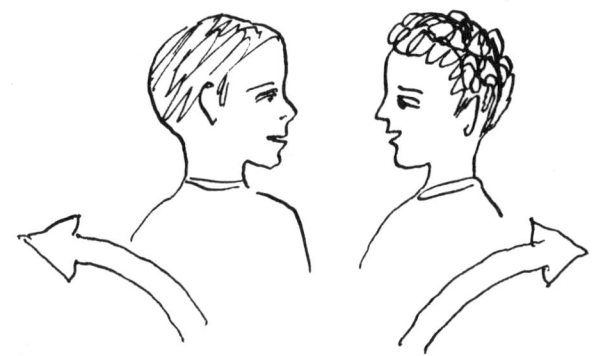

PARTING WITH YOUSEK

I wanted to leave France as soon as possible and get to Gibraltar to rejoin the Allied Forces. Would Yousek go with me now that he was free? I found him sleeping in the train compartment. "Yousek," I said, shaking him awake. "I'm going to Marseille. Later I'll try to find a way to get to Gibraltar. You don't have to go with me. In Auch, you'll be comparatively safe. I heard there are a group of Poles there. You could join them."

    He thought a while. "I think I'll stay in France," he said. At that moment neither of us could know that his freedom would last longer than mine. "Well, take care of yourself, Yousek," I told him. "After what we've been through, the rest should be easy."

    I find it difficult to describe my relationship with Yousek. One would think that, after going through all those life-threatening situations together, we would have developed a profound bond of friendship. Why didn't I feel this? To start with, I didn't have very much in common with Yousek before our escape. He was not a person with whom I could share my thoughts and feelings. Though he was a few years older than I (when we started our escape he was 22 and I was 19), he had asked to join me. I felt flattered, but the fact is I hardly knew him.

Yousek proved later that he was in need of leadership. He also turned out to be a liability. Despite the fact that he had physical stamina, I always had to look out for his well-being, which, naturally, affected my own. I constantly had to check out his camouflage and give him instructions on how to proceed or to hide.

He basically relied on only two things: his prayer book and my leadership. I felt used and angry during those moments when, having enough problems with my own survival, I also had to be responsible for him. However, looking back on it now, I feel this may have been one of the very reasons for my success.

It was a turnabout from my first escape, where I was inadequate to take care of only myself. In becoming a leader for someone else, I had to accept myself in that role and see myself as capable and worthwhile. "Yousek," I used to scold him, "put away your little prayer book and open your eyes instead. You need to become invisible, because if they find you, they will find me, too."

Despite his negatives, I liked Yousek, and, even though it angered me, I accepted his dependence on me. I didn't realize until much later that, at those very moments —indeed, because of them—I was finally growing into manhood.

I got off the train at Lyon and soon picked up one for Marseille. Then I had a problem with the train conductor, who demanded that I show him my ticket. I went through the motions of looking in my pockets and declared that I must have lost it. By the time our disagreement culminated, we had arrived in Marseille and I managed to get away.

As I walked through the railroad station, I worried that I had no money to make a telephone call. This was a ridiculous situation. I should have asked my acquaintance on the train to let me have some pocket money. Well, I thought, I'll have to think of something. After walking for several blocks, I noticed a small church. At the same time, down a nearby alley, I saw a pack of hungry dogs scavenging for food amid overturned garbage pails. Marseille was a hungry city. There was hardly anything in the shops. All the available food was confiscated and sent to Germany. Later I heard that the French had to butcher the zoo animals for meat. The dogs saw me and raced after me, barking and yapping. Just in time I saw a small wrought-iron gate. I ducked in and slammed it shut behind me. Then I shouted and cursed at the dogs. Someone obviously heard the racket, for a few moments later a black-robed priest came out of the church and joined me in hollering at the dogs.

"Oh, Father," I asked. "May I come in? I must use your telephone. You see, I am a Polish POW running from the Germans. It is very important." The priest smiled at my fractured French and said, *"Les Boche sont la meme chose que les chiens la bas* (The Germans are the same as the dogs over there)." He guided me through the dark and empty church to a small adjoining room. Then he pointed to a phone on the desk and said, *"Voila."* As I dialed, I covered the numerals with my arm.

"Hello," I heard a male voice say.

"I must see the captain," I said. "I'm his cousin. Can you take me to him?"

There was a moment of silence. Then another voice got on the line and inquired in Polish, *"O co chodzi* (What's this all about)?" I explained the situation. Someone covered the mouthpiece, and I could hear voices, but not their words. Then the Polish-speaking man returned to the line and said, "Wait near Chat Noir Cafe in Port Vieux at 3 p.m. Walk limping."

"I will," I replied, and hung up. Then I turned to the priest and said, *"Merci beaucoup, et vive la France!"* Once outside, I looked around and saw that it was a nice sunny day with a cool breeze blowing in from the Mediterranean.

FALSE IDENTITY

I checked the time on the church tower's clock. I had an hour to kill. By merely walking south, I came to Port Vieux, the old port. I looked at the old-fashioned schooners and fishing boats moored at the pier. I found the Chat Noir Cafe and remembered to limp. At precisely 3 p.m. a man in fisherman's clothes brushed past me. I followed him, leaving a fair distance between us. He led me for several blocks and finally, glancing at me over his shoulder, stopped at a two-story house that had a second-hand furniture store at street level. I followed him into a dark corridor and up some stairs to the second floor.

A door opened and we entered a comfortable living room. There was the captain, my cousin, enveloped in a cloud of cigar smoke, sitting on a sofa, feet propped up, fingering a glass of Calvados.

"So, here you are, my cousin soldier!" he shouted as he stood up, embracing me. "I'm truly pleased that you made it. I want to hear your story, but first let's have a drink." He poured a Calvados for me. *"Na zdrowie,"* he toasted as he tapped his glass against mine. Then, composing himself again on the sofa, he said, "I knew you were coming. Our man spotted you on the train. Unbelievable coincidence!" He was a big fellow with a glowing red face and penetrating eyes. "Soldier," he said, quickly restoring the military distance between us, "let's talk." Even in civilian garb, he was still a military superman, a professional warrior. He had not been captured in the Valley of St. Die as I had. He was too clever for that. He told me that he had managed to slip out from between the German troops that surrounded the French Army and his Polish division of Grenadiers. I was angry that he had abandoned us, but I thought that confronting him at that moment would be counterproductive.

I explained my situation and brought him up to date on my current status. He listened carefully. Then he turned to a man sitting at a small desk nearby and gave him instructions.

"We're going to give you false I.D. papers," my cousin explained. "These will enable you to be demobilized in Auch. Your identity will be that of a French sergeant released from a German POW camp. You'll get retroactive pay for a year and a half," he said, smiling, "which will amount to a nice sum of money. It'll be paid by the corrupt government of Petain. However," he laughed, "this money will not warm your hand for long. It will be immediately collected by our agent for Underground activities. In return, we shall deliver you to Gibraltar in one of two ways." He paused, giving me a chance to take all of this in. "You could stay in Marseille and work in a salt-processing plant. In time you'd be sent out on a fishing boat that would intercept a British submarine going to

Gibraltar. I warn you, though—the list of men who want this option is very long. It could take some time." He took a swig of his drink. "Your other choice is this. We'd send you to Perpignan, and Spanish smugglers would be paid to deliver you to the British Consulate in Barcelona. With this option, you could start very soon. I don't think you should have any problem crossing the Pyrenees into Spain." I knew immediately that the latter would be my choice.

My cousin exhaled a cloud of cigar smoke, poured another glass of Calvados and proposed a toast. "*Jeszcze Polska nie zginela* (Poland is not lost yet)," he said. We touched glasses and emptied them in one gulp. In the meantime, the man at the desk worked on my documents and snapped my picture for my I.D. card. "For the next couple of days," my cousin said, "you'll be Sergeant Francois Gillet."

"But how can I impersonate a French sergeant?" I asked worriedly. "I can barely speak French!"

"Don't worry," he reassured me. "This demobilization center is entirely in our hands. No one will ask you any questions."

Then he wanted to hear the details of my escape. When I had told my story, he said, "Good job, soldier. Soon you'll be fighting Nazis again. That's what we are here for."

"By the way," I told him. "I need some pocket money." It was given to me together with my new I.D. documents. Another shot of Calvados, and we shook hands good-bye.

It was evening when I caught a train for Auch, and early the next morning I arrived at the demobilization center. It consisted of several military barracks, dismal and depressing in the gray morning. Well, I thought, I won't be staying here for long. I found the main office and registered in my new name. Then, exhausted, I fell asleep in one of the barracks.

The next day I became ill with diarrhea. I stayed at

the center several days. Finally, when my turn came, the office clerks didn't even ask me any questions. They glanced at and retained my new papers. Then they had me sign a receipt for a large amount of money in the form of a check, which was passed directly to the Underground agent. He, in turn, instructed me to join a group of Poles working on a nearby farm. I was to wait there until my departure for Spain. I inquired about Yousek and was told that he was with another group of Polish refugees working on another farm.

Finally, I recalled my promise to the French family and wrote a postcard to Marie, Renee and Andre. *Greetings from a very pleasant vacation. Feeling fine.— Georgette.* I closed my eyes and could see their smiling, happy faces as they read this news.

WAITING

While at the farm in Auch, I met two young Polish men who had managed to avoid capture by the Germans. They were also waiting to cross the Pyrenees into Spain. Like me, they wanted to join the Allied Forces at Gibraltar. Tad, a little older than I, was a vigorous sportsman, very cheerful and likable, a blond man with the physique of an athlete. He was from Gdynia, where I had gone to high school. Tad was a longshoreman and an avid basketball player.

The other fellow, Franciszek, was also older, a few years my senior. Franek, as we called him, had been a barber in prewar Poland. He was a tall man with a mop of brown hair, always smiling or laughing, always entertaining us with his jokes. We spent a lot of time together waiting for transport.

Finally, one day we were told to board a bus for

Goudarque de Gar, where a Polish farm workers' refugee camp was located. We were in very good spirits. Nowadays I often hear that it's healthy to laugh. I remember that we laughed at Franek's jokes for the couple of hours it took to get to our destination, which was a large whitewashed farmhouse converted into dormitories for about two dozen Polish workers who performed various chores at the farm. After checking in, we were permitted to remain idle until our departure for Spain.

SPANISH STING

Finally, after several days of waiting, we were loaded into a windowless van and driven close to the Spanish border near Perpignan. Here we hid in the bushes, waiting for our two Spanish guides. It was getting dark and chilly when they suddenly appeared, like ghosts from out of nowhere. They both wore ponchos made from shabby blankets. On their feet were *appargatas*, shallow sandals made of straw. Their faces looked wild, overgrown with kinky stubble, and over their shoulders they carried bags of contraband. Standing there before us, leaning on their long sticks, they reminded me of two shepherds from the Nativity scene.

    I couldn't understand a word they spoke, but they motioned us to follow them. We traveled up and down a narrow path through the mountains As we emerged from behind some massive rocks, a cold, sharp wind blew and snow started falling. It became more difficult to follow our guides, who moved ahead of us quickly, like mountain goats. We walked carefully as the wind whipped past our ears in violent gusts, blasting icy little snowflakes into our faces.

It is difficult to estimate the length of time passing when every step, every moment, requires one's total attention. Perhaps what felt like an hour could have been a brief minute. The path was so narrow it was barely wide enough for one person. We walked one behind another. The first to follow the smugglers was Tad; I was second, and bringing up the rear and cursing his way through was Franek. At times I looked to one side of our path and fear gripped me as I saw the steep slope of an abyss. The smugglers, of course, knew their way very well. Finally, they led us to a cave where we were to spend the rest of the night.

The cave served only as a primitive shelter from the foul weather. We sat on a cold rock and tried to rest. After a while we ate some of the bread rations we had taken along. Intermittently, we dozed.

At sunrise, we started out again. I looked around and exclaimed to my colleagues: "Hey, Tad, Franek. I'll bet you've never seen a more beautiful view." Indeed, the mountain peaks were bathed in the rosy light of daybreak. The snowy slopes reflected the early morning sun in a million flickering sparkles. It was a breathtaking sight, and it brought me close to a prayer of thanksgiving for the beauty of nature. I felt as if I were in a secret cathedral that enveloped the whole world with love. And yet, I thought, was it on a morning such as this that Cain slew his brother, Abel? Was it also at such a moment that Abraham raised his dagger above the heart of Isaac? Was I not on my way to fight the Nazis? Why do people have to be so cruel to one another? These thoughts were on my mind as we descended the mountain and entered a valley.

We walked for several hours. The sun hadn't yet

reached its zenith when we saw a long stretch of bamboo thicket where the smugglers indicated we should rest.

Just as we started to settle down, one of them produced a revolver. He aimed it at us while the other let loose a torrent of orders, supplemented by mime. To our shock and surprise, we quickly understood that we were to hand over any money we had. I didn't have any, but Tad and Franek gave him theirs. With that, our guides, who turned out to be treacherous crooks, took off, leaving us to our own resources.

There we were, stranded and penniless, unable to speak the language, in a strange country—a hostile, Fascist country to boot!

While talking things over, we realized that, from the outset, our goal had been to get to the British Consulate in Barcelona. Despite our abandonment, we were determined to accomplish just that.

"First, let's get out of here fast," I said. "I feel these guys may sell us to the Spanish police."

"You're right," Tad replied. "Let's hide over there behind those boulders."

We found a good observation place and, without being seen, we could take in everything around us. After a couple of hours we spotted two uniformed policemen. They went straight for the bamboo thicket, obviously looking for us. They searched around but eventually gave up and left. Faraway down the road we could hear them start their car and drive away.

DUNGEONS OF SPAIN

We waited until dark before starting on our way, walking south all through the night. Eventually we emerged on a dirt road that led to Figueras.

By daybreak we saw that we were in the company of several peasants, some in horsecarts, some walking or riding bicycles. As we approached a bridge spanning a river and leading to town, the traffic became congested. At the far end of the bridge, scrutinizing the traffic, was a uniformed guard. I tried to blend in with the peasants. As I walked, I held onto a horsecart, trying to stay out of the policeman's sight. He stood there, clothed in a black cape, shiny black leather leggets and a Napoleon-like three-cornered hat. Later I was told he was one of the dreaded elite police, the Guardia Civil. Just as we thought we might pass through undetected, he saw us. There was a commotion, and I tried to run. A gunshot rang out. We were captured and arrested. Another guard appeared, and we were handcuffed and led to the town's prison.

Figueras prison was very old. It hadn't changed much in 300 years. My cell was a dark dungeon, furnished with only a sack of straw to sleep on. In one corner were two clay jars, one for water, the other for urine. Twice a day we were escorted to the latrine. The iron door of my cell had a spy window, and the only other window was a small one with bars high up near the ceiling. At night the walls were alive with bedbugs, and their bites were like sharp jabs from a hot needle. It was impossible to sleep.

The next day we were interrogated, and my buddies and I were separated. Now I shared a cell with two Spaniards. A few days later, the door opened and another prisoner was pushed in. Shortly afterward, I was told by my Spanish cellmates to watch my words, because the new man was an informer. It is amazing how well one can communicate in sign language.

After several days, I was sent to another prison, in Gerona. It was there that I started to learn Spanish. In order to entertain myself and help pass the many tedious hours, I devised a game. I would conceal a pin in the loose straw on the floor of my cell, and then I would try to find it. I played this game for hours. I also meditated a lot, losing myself in thoughts about my life, my family and the world. I had never found any solace from praying to God. I felt I had to rely on myself.

The prison guards were very rough. They pushed me around, frequently dealing out a blow or a kick. At times I felt I was going crazy in that filthy, depressing environment. I hoped they wouldn't keep me there long.

After several days I was taken to a third prison, this time in Barcelona. There the conditions weren't as ancient, but the treatment was much worse.

I was fascinated by the Spanish people I encountered. My sign language was gradually changing into Spanish. It was becoming easier for me to carry on a conversation with other prisoners. I met many old-timers, imprisoned since the Spanish Civil War. Some of them greeted me with a raised, clenched fist and were very friendly. They were there for being Communists. One day on the way to the latrine, one of them showed me the front page of a Spanish newspaper. The headlines told about Pearl Harbor. America was declaring war against Germany and Japan. We cheered, feeling the war would be over soon.

Finally, I was taken to a fourth prison, a very nasty one in Zaragossa, where the cells were overcrowded to the bursting point. At mealtime, the food was practically thrown at us. The prisoners, many of them without bowls or spoons, tried to catch the soup with their hats or empty sardine cans, or even with their hands. Some, using clam shells, scooped the soup off the dirty floor. Every evening we lined up in our cells for the head count. We were forced to shout "Franco" three times. Those who didn't comply had their faces slapped. Then, just before Christmas, I found myself on a train transport to the Spanish concentration camp Miranda de Ebro.

Not many people outside Spain knew that General Franco maintained several concentration camps for the enemies of his regime as well as of Hitler's. Spain's official status was neutral, and keeping citizens of other sovereign nations as prisoners was in direct violation of international al law.

While at the Zaragossa train station whom should I see, also in the hands of the Guardia Civil, but my buddies from the Pyrennes, Tad and Franek! I shouted to them in Polish: "It's almost a month since I saw you. Are you O.K?" They looked terribly haggard, unshaven and starved. "We learned the Spanish are dirty, uncivilized bastards," Franek cursed. "Look at the cheap sons of bitches. They chained us by the legs because they're short of handcuffs." Then the guard, who of course didn't understand Polish, yelled out, "*Silencio!*" and pushed them onto the train.

It was a long, slow journey. Now I, too, was chained by the leg, to a Frenchman, whereas most of the other prisoners were handcuffed.

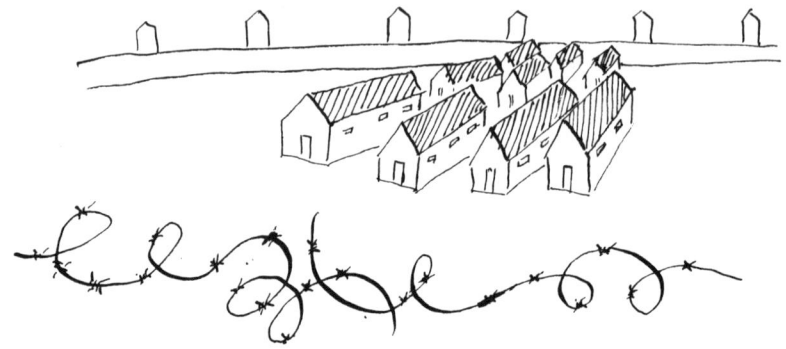

MIRANDA CONCENTRATION CAMP

It was a cold day in December. I was lucky to have a sweater, which I had acquired in France. When we finally arrived at our destination, we marched through a little town and stopped before a barbed-wire gate with the inscription: *todo por la patria*. This was the infamous concentration camp Miranda de Ebro. As the gates of the camp closed behind me, I realized that it was Christmas Day, 1941. I had been free for less than two months.

Soon we were standing at the roll-call plaza, waiting to be counted. It was still afternoon, yet darkness had already started to pervade the gray sky. Gusts of wind carried fine, powder snowflakes, which felt like little burning sparks on my face. I looked around. There in four rows stood whitewashed barracks with red-tiled roofs. The camp was enclosed by a high wall, reinforced both inside and out with fences of barbed wire.

The wall bristled with patrol guards pacing back and forth along its perimeter. A large group of Poles was already in the camp, and Franek, Tad and I were assigned to a Polish barracks, No. 22.

The barracks consisted of two floors. I was given a straw bag to sleep on and a space three feet by eight feet on an upper tier, which could be reached only by a primitive ladder. Tad and Franek were given two spaces nearby.

Edwardo was the capo of my barracks. He was a young man of 20, yet prematurely old, a Polish refugee from France who had spent a considerable amount of time in Spanish prisons, where he had learned to speak the language fluently. He was a sort of liaison officer between the camp authorities and the Polish prisoners.

I met many Poles there from various walks of life. I realized we were in a hostile country, where the dictatorial regime and political sentiments were close to Hitler's. Franco's government, despite its official neutrality, cooperated with the Nazis. That's why we were kept there in such uncivilized conditions. I thought about that as I lay on my sack of straw, covered only with my coat and shivering in the cold winter night. However, it seemed to me that I had gone through the worst back in the German POW camp. I had faith in myself now. I knew I would survive.

I was alert and curious about the camp. It was easier to get world news here than in Germany. I heard that the Germans had suffered from British bombardments and were showing the first signs of defeat. Soon we shall win this war, I thought.

At night I heard the heavy snoring of my companions. The air stank with the odors of unwashed bodies and the stench of decay, odors so indigenous to the overcrowded prisons and POW camps I had been in. The stillness of the night was punctured by the mournful cries of the guards from their sentry boxes: "*Alerta-a-a-a!*" These commands grew louder and louder as they passed along the wall from one guard to another. Then they trailed off into a distant part of the camp.

    I thought of my family. I'll write to them tomorrow, I told myself. Yes, I concluded, we shall survive this war. With that, I fell asleep.

LIFE BEHIND THE WALLS

The morning exploded with a blast from the reveille trumpet. "Everything here is preceded by the sound of that damned horn," one of the old-timers explained to me. We scrambled down from our bunks and ran outside to stand *a la cola* (in line) for ersatz coffee and a slice of hard black bread. With another blast of the trumpet, the kitchen orderly dipped his ladle into the steaming cauldron. Shortly after, yet another trumpet blast announced roll call, followed by *la bandera* (a marching and saluting procedure), on the main plaza. We were ordered to stand in three rows spaced at arm's distance. A Spanish sergeant and his assistants counted the prisoners. The assistants were ready to deal anyone a blow with a rifle butt if the sergeant was displeased.

      The Spanish soldiers looked like strange, tattered

vagabonds. They wore loose hanging ponchos, *appargatas* and pants narrowing like leggings with unbuttoned flaps. On their heads sat shallow caps with front and rear horns. From the front horn hung a red fuzzy pompon, which swung in front of the soldier's eyes with each head movement. I never found out the purpose of this strange device. Perhaps such annoying interference with his vision was supposed to trigger off in the man a state of frenzy when confronted with an enemy, as in a *corrida*, when a bull is brought to rage by being jabbed with *banderillas*. These soldiers looked shabby and were shabbily treated by their officers. The soldiers, in turn, abused the prisoners, who were at the bottom of the hierarchy.

After the head count and at the trumpet's signal, we marched to *la bandera*, the raising-of-the-flag routine. To the sound of a military march, sometimes *Stars and Stripes Forever*, played by a prisoners' band, we were ordered to stand in three-abreast formation while a Spanish officer raised the flag. Then the band changed the tune. They played *Roquete*, then two anthems, first the royalist, then the Falangist. Everyone *had* to sing, and the soldiers watched each man's mouth. After the singing an officer shouted, *"Espana,"* and we all had to respond, *"Grande!"* Again *"Espana,"* and we had to answer *"Libre."* Then he would yell, *"Viva Espana!"* to which we had to answer *"Viva!"* Finally he yelled, *"Viva Franco!"* and we had to shout three times: *"Franco! Franco! Franco!"*

We got our revenge here, because instead of shouting "Franco," we shouted *"Sram go,"* which sounded similar but when translated into vulgar Polish means "Shit on him." I'm sure the Spaniards could never understand why the Polish group shouted the last part of this ritual so vehemently.

Taking down the flag in the evening required the same procedure. Once a week we were also subjected to the rigors of *la bandera grande*, which had the additional feature of tricky marching in front of General Franco's monument. Forcing prisoners to actively participate in glorifying this Fascist dictator was in direct violation of the Geneva Convention. In this as well as in many other aspects of abuse, the Spanish guards proved to be vicious and barbaric in dealing with us.

Time passed slowly, but we rejoiced at the news that the Nazis were losing the war. To fill up our time, the guards made us carry rocks from one side of the camp to the other, and then back again, whipping us with sticks along the way. After all I had been through, though, I didn't find this chore that painful. We were constantly subjected to lengthy roll calls and stood in ranks for hours while the tedious task of counting heads went on. Often the guards found someone they disliked, and he would be dealt a few blows and sent to *calaboso* (solitary confinement).

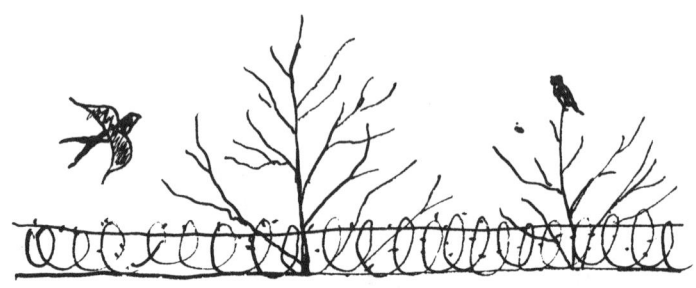

SOME TRIED

Despite the fact that Miranda was well guarded, there were several escape attempts. Once during the delivery of potatoes to the kitchen, a prisoner managed to get close to the truck. Unnoticed, he crawled under and strapped himself to the undercarriage. He left the gate this way and was never heard from again. In another case, a prisoner very carefully observed the behavior of the Guardia Civil official in charge of the camp's files. The official's office was in a building close to the gate. Every day, very punctually, this man left his office at five minutes to five. Since he was recognized on sight, the gate was immediately opened for him. This routine went on day after day, for months. One day our observant prisoner managed to get close to the gate under cover of darkness. He wore an imitation of

SOME TRIED

Guardia Civil garb, which he had very patiently created out of scraps of various materials. He carried a bogus briefcase made out of cardboard to still his shaking hands. It was about seven minutes to five when, without any questions, the gate was opened for him. And so, having two minutes' gain on his potential pursuers, he bolted swiftly away from the camp. The rest of the story became known to us because it was told to us directly by him. After a few weeks he was brought back to the camp minus a leg. He had lost it while trying to board a freight train.

Another foiled attempt at escape occurred when a prisoner struck a deal with a guard and paid the guard handsomely for allowing him to climb over a wall. The prisoner shouldn't have trusted him. The guard shot the man dead in cold blood.

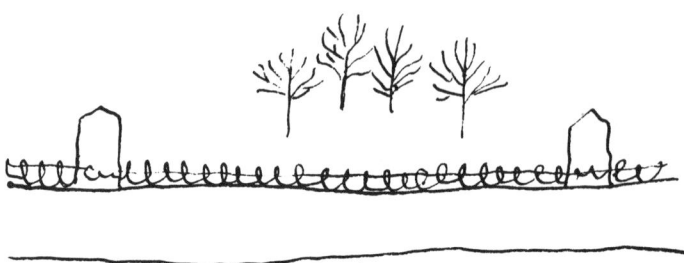

TUNNEL

At this time there was an atmosphere of secrecy in the Polish barracks, because we, too, were preparing an escape from the camp by digging a tunnel that would lead under and past the wall. We had excellent human resources for this purpose; among us were engineers, an architect and very determined diggers.

Digging was easy in the beginning, but later, after we made some progress, being underground was like being in a coffin. Sometimes I was on the verge of panic. What if I get cut off by sliding earth? I thought. I was probably not the only one who felt such fear, because soon it was decided to make the tunnel wider and support it with lumber. I dug with a metal food can and piled the soil under my belly. Then I managed to drop it and pushed it behind me

TUNNEL

with my feet. Someone in back of me then pulled the dirt, with a can fastened to a long stick, toward the entrance. There the dirt was placed in small bags to be ready for spreading outside, but spreading very carefully so as not to attract attention. Usually the bag was carried under someone's belt and the dirt let out through the bottom of the trousers. This dug-up dirt was dispersed near the latrines. Working very slowly and with the participation of at least a dozen prisoners, we took about four weeks to reach the wall. We celebrated this event silently.

Piotr was finally chosen to break through. He was a very strong young man and eager to make the first break. A long rope was attached to his belt. It was agreed that, when he got out, he would pull on the rope to help the others clear the tunnel in a hurry. My turn was No. 7. We were all ready to go when suddenly we heard several shots, one after another. There was a tugging on the rope, and now our roles were reversed. We were frantically pulling Piotr back in. Out of breath and bleeding, Piotr was finally pulled out from the tunnel. Fortunately, his arm had only a superficial wound. In a moment we camouflaged everything as much as possible and dispersed. In a few minutes, we heard the commands for a roll call. We found out later that Piotr had surfaced directly in the path of a patrolling guard. The astonished guard noticed the hole, stuck his rifle in it and fired several times. Piotr managed to grab the barrel and push it away from himself, thus saving his life. The entrance to the tunnel was discovered and several prisoners found themselves in solitary confinement. Fortunately, I was not one of them. The next day the guards started laying cement floors in all the barracks.

Yet another escape was attempted. We used the same tunnel, after breaking through the cement floor. After this attempt, the floors were carefully inspected once a week, and the solitary confinement cells were never empty.

HUNGER STRIKE

Miranda de Ebro was living proof of the Franco-Hitler alliance. While Spain was officially neutral, Franco did everything in his power to accommodate the Nazis.

Compared to my previous imprisonment by the Nazis, life in Miranda was not as bad. Our treatment was less cruel. In Spain we Poles weren't hated as we were in Germany, although certain guards and officers were vicious. I remember one young Polish officer named Kaminski who was killed in cold blood while trying to escape. Other prisoners were tortured.

The escape path out of Europe through the Pyrenees was well known. Many tried this route, and some made it to the British, Canadian or American consulates. Among them were British pilots shot down over Germany,

HUNGER STRIKE

a large number of civilians running from the Nazis and POW escapees like myself.

I soon learned that some of the prisoners were very rich and ran secret gambling games. For those with money, almost anything could be gotten in the camp. For the others, poor like myself, the days crawled. Someone in the camp had a radio, and we shared the news, expecting the war to end soon. We organized a world affairs forum and had lively discussions concerning our future. There were classes in Spanish, offered by the more qualified inmates, which I attended. Despite the fact that the food was much better than in the POW camps, there was never enough, and we were always hungry.

In January 1943 a group hunger strike was organized. Germany was facing multiple defeats, and in view of that situation Franco was not eager to commit Spain to the war. The organizers of the strike felt it was an opportune time to act.

Meanwhile, after much deliberation, I decided to write a letter to my family. I used the name of a friend to prevent any possible repercussions due to my escape. Several weeks later I received a reply. They wrote that they were all alive and were thinking of me.

YOUSEK AGAIN

More and more prisoners of many nationalities were brought to the camp every day. And each day we waited for the new arrivals, looking for someone we might know. One day a fresh transport of Poles arrived. I could hardly believe my eyes when I saw Yousek among them.

"Yousek!" I yelled from the group of onlookers. He saw me and waved. That evening he told me he had worked on a farm in France all this time. "Lately, though, it's been too dangerous for Poles to live in France," he explained, "so I joined a group that crossed the mountains trying to get into Portugal. We were caught, and I was in a couple of prisons." After a quiet moment, he asked anxiously, "What do you think will happen to us now?"

"I think the war will be over soon, and they will have

YOUSEK AGAIN

to let us out," I said. We reminisced about our escape and talked of our chances in the present situation. By now our Polish group numbered more than 500.

MAIL FROM HOME

One day I received a letter from my sister Viesia, who lived in Warsaw. She wrote that our family was alive and well. They were all concerned about me and sent me their love.

Viesia was four years older than I, and I loved and admired her very much. I loved my four-years-younger sister, Marysia, no less, yet there was something special to me about having an older sibling. Viesia was not only older but also an unusually talented young woman. She was an outstanding student and a fine pianist. I'd always felt that my father wanted me to be more like her. But I was a dreamer, not a scholar. In fact, I was a very mediocre student. Viesia was the best in everything she did. She'd had no difficulty getting a scholarship to medical school and was on her way to becoming a doctor. It is difficult to describe how proud we all were of her. I never blamed her for casting such a large shadow over Marysia and me. We knew we could never match her, so we didn't try.

In order to make the hunger strike a success, we knew we had to obtain international publicity that would expose the existence of this infamous camp and tell of the strike itself. One of the ideas considered was to smuggle someone out of the camp and into Portugal. From there he could alert the International Red Cross and foreign embassies that a hunger strike of several hundred citizens from many sovereign nations was taking place in the concentration camp Miranda de Ebro, thus challenging the neutrality of Spain. One day I heard that a Polish officer had been dispatched from the camp for this very purpose. Apparently he had been concealed in a garbage bag, taken outside the camp and dumped in the Ebro River as part of the routine garbage disposal. He then cut himself loose and swam to freedom. He was successful, because several days later we received a postcard from him from Portugal. I also heard that a large number of mini-balloons had been released one windy night. Each balloon carried a message publicizing the hunger strike in three languages. This may be difficult to believe, but in the camp almost anything could be obtained for money.

The day the hunger strike began, the trumpet blew the usual signal, and we formed the usual line. But as the line moved, everyone just walked by the cauldrons, to the amazement of the Spanish guards. Of course, we had our own militia watching the strikers. No one was allowed to eat!

Several days passed. Initially I suffered great hunger pangs and cramps. By the fifth day I could barely walk and would get dizzy when I passed the cauldrons. On the eighth day an official from the Polish Consulate arrived. He was an emissary of the Polish consul, Szumlakowski, who, we heard, had cooperated with Franco during the civil war and was now Franco's friend. He could have freed the Polish group without difficulty if he had wanted to. He had never done anything for us during our imprisonment, but now, with public opinion alerted, he had no choice in the matter. So he had sent his emissary, in a pretense of concern. Szumlakowski was said to be a fascist and was vehemently hated by all of us. Eventually, the British Embassy intervened, and we were told that we were all going to be freed.

The leaders of the Polish prisoner group, who had organized the hunger strike, deserve much praise. They thought of every detail and served as an example. They pulled the prisoners of other nationalities into the strike and were in large part responsible of its success.

Finally leaving the camp after more than two years of imprisonment was an emotional experience, to say the least. I marvelled at every blade of grass, everything that lived, everything that my eyes could perceive. I wanted to touch all of it to make sure it was real. I could finally see all the trees, not just the tops, which till then had been the only part visible from inside the camp. I used to look for hours at those tree tops, trying to imagine the part hidden by the high wall.

Seeing my camp experience from the outside provided a bitter satisfaction. My years of detention had not all been a deficit, I realized. Besides learning Spanish, I had learned a great deal about life and people and, most of all, about myself. I'd done a lot of thinking and growing. And I'd always believed one day I would be free.

On the train to Madrid we sang and laughed and celebrated our freedom, drinking wine provided by our British liberators.

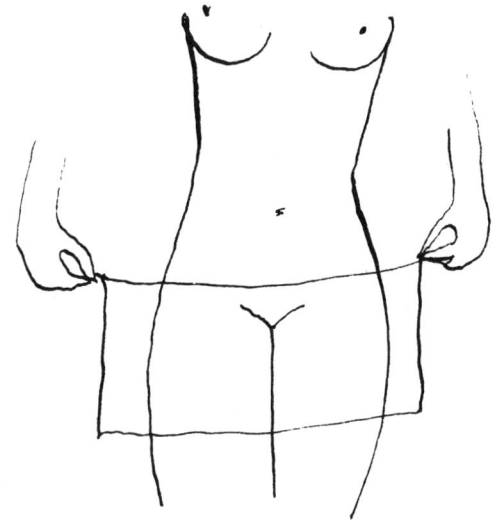

MADRID

It was the spring of 1943 in Madrid. We relished our newly found freedom. Tad, Franek and I now resided at the Pension Castillo in the center of town. We were allotted a generous amount of pocket money and had our living expenses paid for by the British Embassy. While awaiting a transport for Gibraltar, I explored the city, enjoying my freedom. For me El Prado Museum was a favorite place, because I had been interested in art ever since I was a small child.

It was very early in my life when I first remember sitting on the floor, holding a crayon in my hand and drawing pictures on paper. Later, I recall frequent visits to the studio of Felix Zawirsky, a dear friend of my parents who was a noted Polish painter and lived nearby. Fascinated, I spent hours watching him at his easel. He encouraged me to paint with watercolors. I think he would be pleased with my work today if he were still alive. Unfortunately, he was shot dead in the first days of the Nazi invasion when he answered the doorbell of his studio and was murdered on the spot by a Nazi soldier who thought all Polish intellectuals should be annihilated.

I was encouraged by my mother, who never missed an opportunity to point out to me the beauty of nature. I spent a considerable amount of time peering into the blossoms of flowers, observing with great curiosity their various shapes and colors and the activity of the nectar-gathering insects. At other times, with my face submerged in the water of a nearby pond, I would watch the secret life going on there. My drawings and paintings brought me many compliments, and accordingly, I liked to act in a manner that, to my child's mind, befitted a full-fledged artist. Even though I really enjoyed drawing and painting, my budding ego was in need of praise. I remember a time when I was about seven or eight and had been up in my room working on a watercolor. Unexpectedly, I heard voices and realized some friends of my parents had stopped by for a visit. I quickly smeared some paint on my shirt, dabbing here and there, and then emerged with my painting. They were enchanted, and to this day I remember their remarks: "Just look at this child. He is so little and already an accomplished painter!"

But the single event that determined my career as an artist was the occasion when I was unexpectedly praised by my father. I don't remember him ever saying anything complimentary to me before then—or even after. He was a scholar who had very high academic standards, which I could never meet. But this occasion was different. I was seated at the dining room table, busily drawing a glass bowl filled with apples and pears that was on the table. I was about nine years old. My father walked by, noticed my drawing and stopped. He studied it for a few moments and

MADRID

then exclaimed proudly: "That's very good, Yurek!" Instantly, time stood still. That rare praise had a profound effect on me. I think it was at that moment I decided to become an artist. What a pity my father died before he could see that, 40 years later, my art would be honored by a one-man show that toured several museums throughout Poland.

But that is another story, occurring much later, long after I came to America and finally settled down to study at some of the country's foremost art schools. With each success in my art career, however, I wished my father could have been there.

I was also interested in other aspects of life that came with the precious freedom I had achieved. I wanted to experience life as much as possible, to compensate for all the time I had been imprisoned. And I was not the only one who felt that way. One day Franek, Tad and I were talking. "We have to live well while we can," Franek said. "Who knows what tomorrow will bring?"

"Anything in particular on your mind?" asked Tad.

"As a matter of fact, yes," Franek replied. "How would you like to visit a nice little brothel in the neighborhood?"

"Sounds interesting to me!" Tad said, and I agreed.

We counted our money and set out for the red-light district of town. Being the most experienced, Franek led the way.

I was both very nervous and very excited. I had never been to a brothel before; this would be my first experience of adult sex. I imagined myself embracing the nude body of a beautiful woman. I shuddered with delightful expectation. It was the first time in three years that I had even daydreamed of a sexual encounter. Till then I had dreamed mostly of food and freedom. Yet since I was a small child, I seemed to be obsessed with sex, to which I was introduced early in life.

SEX ABUSE AT FOUR

As I looked over my shoulder, searching in that far horizon of my memory, I saw a quiet little village in Poland. This was the landscape of my childhood. Nothing much ever happened here. Time, it seemed, had stopped, and a lazy feeling, like morning mist, hung in the air. It was so quiet you could hear people talking a kilometer away, or dogs barking at a distant farm, or the squeaking of a horse-drawn cart somewhere on a sandy winding road. Across the fields church bells tolled. This little village had no church bells of its own to mind time. All who lived here went about their lives unhurriedly.

Among tall shrubs of lilac and jasmine stood an old brick schoolhouse with its sign painted in large white letters: SZKOLA. This is where I lived and where my parents taught.

The portion of the building that was the school consisted of two large classrooms. In one my mother taught the lower grades. The other, housing the older children, was ruled by my father, the schoolmaster. The remaining part of the building was our home. As additional privileges, the county provided such a teaching family with a barn, a stable, a woodshed and gardens. Our flower garden was at the front entrance and a vegetable garden and an orchard were at the rear of the property. We also had an acre of grain fields and a meadow, which provided hay for our cow and goats. In addition, we kept ducks, geese and chickens.

For ornamental purposes, two peacocks graced our property. They would emit eerie, mournful shrieks at the least expected moments in that idyllic solitude.

Having so much to take care of, my parents employed a handyman and a maid. Bogusia, the nursemaid, took care of me while my parents taught classes. She was a young peasant girl of 14 with a pleasant voice. She had blue eyes and blonde hair, into which she wove field flowers. Bogusia and I spent a lot of time together. She sang lullabies and folk songs to me. She cuddled and kissed me, hugging me to her little breasts.

Somewhere in the playground of my childhood a currant bush grows. It sparkles with translucent ruby-red berries in the hot summer afternoon. At four, I was small enough to see those berries above my head. Some touched my cheek. I stretched upward and plucked them off with my lips. They quenched my thirst on a hot day. The currant bush is still very important to me because it reminds me of Bogusia.

It was a hot afternoon in June. Bogusia and I hid in the garden in the shade of the overhanging branches. We lay on a blanket spread over soft, aromatic grasses. It was very quiet there except for the chorus of children's voices in the distance reciting in monotonous unison the letters

SEX ABUSE AT FOUR

of the alphabet. From time to time my mother's voice rose above the children's and dominated this litany. Bees buzzed about, feeding on the sweet nectar of the flowers. Time stood still.

The coolness of the shade and the laziness of the afternoon made us drowsy. Bogusia caressed and kissed me all over. She took off my shorts and kissed my belly, then all the way down to my knees. She took my hand and pulled me toward her. Then she guided my hand slowly up her leg. I saw she wore nothing under her skirt. I remember being curious and I explored with interest that part of her body I had never seen before. Then Bogusia opened her legs and guided my hand to her pink, moist lips. She sighed with pleasure, and I, surprised at the effect of my touch, doubled my efforts and played her like a harp.

After a while, Bogusia picked several currants and placed them within her pink lips. She leaned toward me and whispered in my ear that I should pluck them out with my tongue and mouth. She said she was curious if I would be able to get them out this way and eat them.

It was not an easy game. Bogusia made it more difficult for me by wiggling her belly.

After a while, I was able to get a few and crunch them in my teeth. I tried for more. Suddenly Bogusia began to wiggle more rapidly. She trembled and pushed my face into her with both hands. I struggled for air and almost suffocated. I tore myself away from her and began to cry. She kissed me and promised not to play that game anymore.

The sex games I played with Bogusia remained our special secret. Somewhere at the edge of my memory I can still see a currant bush sparkling with ruby-red berries in the lazy hot afternoon. In its shade a young girl whispers in a little boy's ear: "Keep making nice to Nanny."

That was my first introduction to sex, one of the earliest memories of my childhood. Later, growing older, I remembered with fascination that sexual experience.

Suddenly the flow of my memories was interrupted as Tad and Franek turned into a doorway and I followed them upstairs. We entered a large room. My nostrils filled with an exotic perfume. A number of overpainted and underdressed young women sat on couches, smoking cigarettes. They greeted us cheerfully, and some of them paraded in front of us in a sexy, provocative manner. Others tried to sit on our laps, teasing us and smiling. Finally, we each chose a partner and, after paying the madam in advance, we followed the girls to their rooms.

"What's your name?" I asked the girl I had chosen. "Nieves," she replied. She was a small, shapely young woman, with long black hair and a pretty smile. She walked over to a mirrored makeup table, opened a drawer and handed me a condom. Then she undid her scanty dress, which fell to the floor, and stood nude in front of me.

I feasted my hungry eyes on her insolent smile, her beautiful breasts, her smooth, flat belly, and the triangle of black fur between her white thighs. A delicious shudder ran down my spine. Suddenly I was holding her close to me, and, like a blind man, I felt the shape of her body with my probing, caressing hands.

We fell on a bed amid waves of a musical crescendo that was pulsating in my ears, and . . . in a minute it was all over. In another minute Nieves, her dress already back on, was guiding me out of the room. "I must see you again," I implored. "I'll take you to lunch and we'll go to El Prado together."

But Nieves said she never went out with anyone during the day. "If you want to be with me longer, you have to pay Madam for the whole night."

I hurriedly said, "Then I'll do just that." But as it turned out, I didn't have enough money. So I waited till the next week's allowance from the British Embassy. Then I rushed to see Nieves again. I was so intoxicated and enamored of her that I even told her I'd marry her if she'd stop seeing other men. She only laughed at me.

It was a few weeks later when Franek brought us the news that we were shipping out to Portugal and then to Gibraltar. I was surprised to realize I was willing to leave Nieves and Madrid with all its attractions. Joining the Allied Forces again became my first priority. The Nazis were losing the war, and I wanted to fight them before everything was all over.

One beautiful day in May, a large group of us Poles boarded a train for Portugal. Tad, Franek and I looked out the windows. As soon as we crossed the Spanish-Portuguese border, we noticed things looked different. The houses in Portugal seemed cleaner and more prosperous, the people more courteous. As much as we detested Fascist Spain, we liked Portugal.

ANTELOPE

Villa Real de San Antonio, a small village on the Atlantic coast, was our destination. It was there, after our arrival, that we awaited sea transport to Gibraltar. I still remember the sounds of the musical horn of the British Embassy's limousine, darting to and fro as it went about the business of providing accommodations and food for our group.

The next morning I remember as the most beautiful I had seen in a long time. We boarded some fishing dories and set out for the edge of territorial waters. There we saw the British destroyer HMS *Antelope* waiting for us. As we approached the ship, we heard its bullhorn welcoming us aboard in the name of King George. High swells tossed the dories up and down as we groped for the rope ladders and pulled ourselves up onto the huge warship.

The British sailors were very hospitable. They

offered us food, candy and cigarettes. I stood on the destroyer's deck and let the wind and salty spray kiss my face as the ship, going full speed, cut like a knife through the sapphire waters of the Atlantic.

At that moment I felt totally free and aware of the power in myself to protect my freedom. Behind me lay three years of imprisonment, abuse and hunger. Even though it was getting dark, I stayed on deck, my face wet with sea spray. I let myself wonder if this was just one of those dreams I had dreamed behind the barbed wires. I realized then that I had always known it would end this way, that one day I would again live in peace and have a family to whom I would tell all about my experiences and how sweet freedom is.

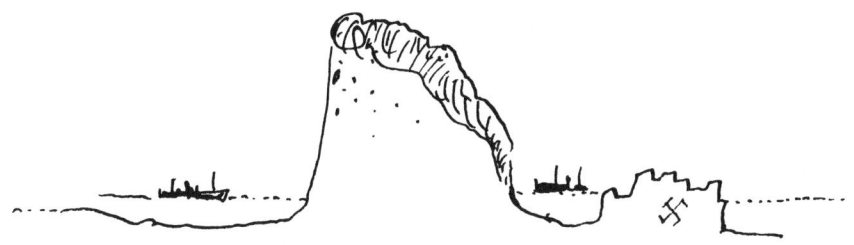

GIBRALTAR AT LAST

Gibraltar was an anthill of soldiers, bristling with heavy guns embedded into fortifications cut into the rock. Nearby, on Spanish soil, forming a small peninsula, lay Algeciras, a Nazi spy outpost, where, with General Franco's permission, the Germans observed every movement of the Allies' ships.

    We stayed in Gibraltar just long enough to exchange our civilian garb for khaki military uniforms. After a short respite, we boarded the British transport *City of Norwich* to leave "the Rock" for England. We were part of an unusually large convoy of about 80 ships that had assembled at Gibraltar. Our movements were carefully watched by the Germans at Algeciras. Consequently, the ships moved back and forth as in a chess game, trying to disguise their purpose and direction. Then one night, under cover of darkness, the whole convoy slipped out into the Atlantic.

ESCAPE INTO DANGER

The *City of Norwich* was a large freighter that had been converted into a troop ship and carried close to a thousand men. As I stepped down into the cavernous hold, I was amazed to see a vast jungle of hammocks swinging from side to side with every movement of the ship.

The convoy moved north like a large herd of sheep, flanked by swift, watchful Navy destroyers running here and there like dogs keeping the herd together and safe.

We were getting close to Biscay Bay. The Atlantic was calm, yet our ship swayed from side to side as the western wind pushed the swells on harborside. Yousek, Franek, Tad and I took off our shirts and lay on the deck, drinking in the sun. Tad felt seasick and kept throwing up over the side. Franek, feeling fine, kept us in stitches, telling one joke after another. I looked around and saw the horizon filled with ships. I thought the convoy must be carrying close to a hundred thousand men. It was May 1943. The Nazis were losing the war. We listened to the news and cheered. In the meantime, there was nothing to do but relax and get a nice tan.

Suddenly someone yelled out, "Listen to that!" Sure enough, we heard the distant rattling of anti-aircraft weapons and the sound of explosions. Then we heard a faint drone and saw a German plane hovering high over our convoy. At that moment, alarm sirens sounded. Someone shouted, "Everyone down below, on the double!" The piercing sounds of the sirens continued as we scrambled down the metal ladders into the cavernous holds. Soon we were crowded together as if in a coffin. We knew we were being attacked by German planes.

In another moment, all hell broke loose. Our ship shook in a paroxysm of anti-aircraft gunfire. From the ship's belly we heard our machine guns firing frantically. I looked around and saw hundreds of pairs of eyes distorted with fear, hundreds of clenched fingers grasping anything or anyone to keep balance. All around us was pandemonium and the sounds of rapid firing and explosions. Evidently the entire convoy was fighting for its life as the whine of diving planes added to the cacophony. Our thoughts raced in panic, our hearts in our throats.

Then a heavy explosion told us that we had been hit. The ship shook and listed to port while we panicked, hopelessly trapped below. Fortunately we didn't have to abandon ship, even if that had been possible. We limped on, feeling lucky that it was only a bomb from a plane and not a torpedo. However, at dusk, German submarines attacked and sank some of our ships. The next day, up on deck again, I watched a ship being hit by a torpedo. The ship broke in half, and within two minutes it sank with all aboard. Hundreds of men died. Yet the convoy moved on, and in spite of some damaged ships, including ours, we finally reached England.

Whoever entered England during the war was very carefully screened to prevent enemy infiltration. We were no exception to this rule. That's why, once more, we were locked up in a camp, though this time only for a few days. "Oh, no!" I complained. "Everywhere I go, I get locked up. I've had enough of that for the rest of my life!"

After answering many questions and proving my identity, I was sent to Scotland, where Yousek and I joined a regiment of the Polish Army. Tad enlisted in a paratroop outfit, and Franek went into the armored corps.

My regiment was stationed near the little town of Aberfeldy. Every Friday night there was dancing at a social hall. It was here that I learned to dance, and I dated my pretty dancing partners. There was fierce competition between the Polish and Norwegian soldiers for the friendship of the Scottish girls.

The rest of the time I spent on military training. Yousek and I drove heavy lorries for the transportation of soldiers. We drove in column formation, getting ready for the real thing.

CAPTAIN KOMOROVSKI

Eventually our regiment was involved in war games in Yorkshire. One day our convoy of lorries came to a halt at the periphery of a small town. The soldiers spilled out and set their gear on the ground, then hurried into roll-call formation. Red emblems reading POLAND on our khaki uniforms indicated our origin. All around and through Yorkshire, Polish army units were in training for the impending invasion of Normandy.

Captain Komorovski stepped out of a sleek, sporty Austin and waved off his orderly/chauffeur. The captain, in his middle 50s, was an intensely disliked man because of his nasty disposition and extremely arrogant ways. His haughtiness was accentuated by the way in which he strutted in front of his men, mumbling curses. From under

CAPTAIN KOMOROVSKI

a black, leather-edged beret adorned with a silver Polish eagle and past a fringe of graying hair and bushy, anger-knitted brows gleamed a pair of sadistic eyes. These were set in the beefy countenance of a cruel drunkard. Captain Komorovski was a known alcoholic.

He had been born in Byelorussia, into an old aristocratic family. Some of its members had served the Russian czar as loyal dignitaries. They were hated by the impoverished *kulaks*, the serfs, whom they often oppressed.

During the Russian Revolution, many Komorovskis were lynched. Some took refuge in Poland, where they were placed in the Polish Army as officers. Here they were honored and cherished, because many Poles hated the Bolsheviks.

Now Komorovski stood in front of his company, feet slightly apart, swaying back and forth, cursing his men. The curses he spat out were Russian, not Polish. He used obscene Russian invectives to insult his subordinates, a way of further degrading them. Then, as if he had a need to latch onto someone in particular, he directed a string of those insults at me—and all because of a missing button on my uniform. "Step out, *doorak!*" he ordered. (*Doorak* means "stupid.")

I was not a novice in matters of war, and after all I had been through, I was not going to take those insults lying down. How dare he talk to me that way, I thought, cursing me in Russian as if I were a dog! Oh, how I despised him! Then I suddenly realized whom he reminded me of: the commandant of the POW camp in Germany, herr hauptman Otto Richter. Richter had been prancing the same way in front of our roll-call formation of prisoners when he ordered us to look at the limp body of Edek, and I remembered what had happened to Janek when he averted his eyes. Captain Komorovski might just as well have worn a swastika on his uniform. The way he carried himself, the way he hated, cursed and tried to dehumanize his men, was just like Otto Richter.

A March wind blew in gusts of penetrating chill and made the men shudder. "Step out, *doorak!*" The command echoed in the air.

I stepped out the required five paces in front of the ranks and clicked my heels at attention. Komorovski slowly sauntered over. Very slowly. Then he looked piercingly into my eyes. *"Sobachyi narod!"* he barked in his best Russian. (It was a curse meaning "canine breed.") I tensed and looked into his eyes with such tangible hate that he winced, as if slapped by my venomous gaze.

"Sir, Private Jerzy Iwaszkiewicz, sir," I heard myself saying. "I am in the Polish Army, and you have no right to curse me in your Russian language, sir." Those words, which came out of my mouth loudly and distinctly, surprised even me! To the captain, they must have seemed like a challenge to God himself; to the other men standing there, like an act of sheer insanity.

A deadly silence fell. Even the wind died. The blood drained from Komorovski's face. He appeared to tremble for a moment or two. His hand shot to his side but, fortunately for me, he wasn't carrying a gun. He gasped for air, sputtered incoherently, then screamed at the top of his lungs: "Sergeant of the guard, ARREST THIS MAN!" With that, he abruptly dismissed the company and stormed off.

I was led to the guardhouse while the men congregated and talked in hushed voices.

"I sure thought that sonofabitch Komorovski was going to explode!" someone said. "Did you see him go for his gun?"

"Yurek was lucky," another added. "In the Czar's army they shot you right on the spot for something like that! Officer's honor, you know."

"I never thought Yurek had the guts to stand up to the old bastard," someone else offered.

"It's not guts, it's stupidity! I hope Yurek doesn't

have to rot in the brig till the end of the war," said Antek, who stood near me in formation. He was my close friend.

"Don't worry," Yousek reassured him. "I know him better than any of you. We both escaped from the kraut's camp. This guy is lucky. It's hard to believe what we both pulled through. You'll see. . . he'll get out of this somehow."

The next morning I woke up in the detention cell at the guardhouse. "What are they going to do with me now?" I asked the guard.

"As far as I know," he replied, "you're going to stay here for quite a while. But first I have orders to escort you to roll call. Then the captain himself will tell you where you're going, and for how long."

At roll call I was ordered to stand separately, at the side of the ranks. The company's sergeant went through the orders-of-the-day papers. Then he announced that a volunteer was needed to join the field surgical unit.

The FSU was one of the most dangerous outfits, because it dealt with attending to the wounded under enemy fire.

After making his request, the sergeant looked around at the men standing before him. There was a long silence. Hastily, I made a decision. I stepped out and said, "I wish to be transferred to FSU at your request."

All eyes turned toward me, but especially the captain's. A smirk came over his face. He seemed to be calculating the odds of my demise and appeared appeased by this turn of events.

I was transferred that same day and started rigorous training. When I realized how dangerous my new assignment was, I wondered if I hadn't indeed signed my own death certificate.

Then, unexpectedly, and for no known reason, my entire field surgical unit was dissolved, and I was transferred to the Merchant Marines. In the days and weeks following my transfer, while steaming in convoys around England, I often thought of Yousek and Antek and the others I'd left behind who were still being bullied by the captain.

Shortly after the invasion of Normandy, my ship docked at Dundee, Scotland. I went ashore and started walking through the town. From a distance, I saw a man with crutches leaning against a wall near the entrance to a hospital. There was something familiar about him, and when I got closer I saw it was Antek.

"I can't believe it!" I exclaimed, hugging him. "What happened to you?"

Antek smiled thinly. "As you can see, Yurek," he said, "I'm lucky. I only lost a leg. You're not going to believe what happened." He stopped to compose himself. "Only a few of us survived." Again he fell silent.

"But what *happened?*" I prodded, demanding to know.

Slowly, he told his story. "One night that sonofabitch Komorovski got drunk. He miscalculated and sent our whole column of lorries too far after the Germans. It was the British Air Force that wiped us out. They did a pretty good job of it, too, thinking we were German troops."

"What happened to Yousek?" I demanded.

"Yousek was killed," said Antek softly.

I gasped. How could fate be so cruel? After all we had been through and the war almost over. And now Yousek lay buried somewhere in Normandy. I could hardly believe it.

"And the captain?" I asked.

"Komorovski was lucky," Antek replied. "The old bastard only got a flesh wound. They tried to court-martial him, but he talked his way out of it. But not for long. One of our men got him." Antek sighed. "Remember that young kid who drove his lorry a few spaces behind us? The guy who used to draw pictures? I don't even remember his name. Well, this guy lost his right hand. Shortly after

CAPTAIN KOMOROVSKI

Komorovski was acquitted, this kid waits for him by the officers' latrine. The kid stabbed him so many times some of the guys said there was a stab wound for each man in the company. And he did it with his left hand. He used to draw with his right, but he didn't have that one anymore."

S/S KROSNO

I spent a lot of time thinking about how lucky I was that I'd left Komorovski's unit. It was ironic that, in England, hoping to fight our way back to Poland, we had to fight little dictators like him. The army was full of them. No wonder I'd applied for transfer to the Merchant Marines.

One day I was on a train heading for Glasgow, Scotland, where I was to join the crew of the S/S *Krosno* as an ordinary seaman. I had departed from London, where I'd received my transfer documents. I was glad to be leaving that city, which was under constant air-raid attacks.

Once in Glasgow, I looked for my ship. When I found her, neatly tucked in a corner of the pier, she seemed much smaller than I had expected.

The *Krosno* was a Polish freighter owned by the

Polish Gdynia-American Lines and, like other Allied Merchant Marine ships during the war, was under the supervision of the British Admiralty. Her captain, Boleslaw Mikszta, was Polish, and so was the rest of the crew, except for two British Navy gunners and one Scot, who was a deckhand.

The gangway squeaked and swayed under my weight, and my steps sounded hollow as I walked across the iron deck toward a mumble of voices. When I got to the messroom, I stopped in the doorway. The deck crew was there, busily devouring some roasted chickens. The men looked like a pack of wolves chewing over the carcasses of freshly killed game. Their hands and faces were oily and dripping with fat. They didn't use forks or knives. I entered the room, and for a moment all eyes fastened on me. "I'm the new man," I said, trying to be friendly. They weighed and measured me with their eyes, but they never stopped eating. "I'm the boatswain here," said a short, barrel-chested man with a no-nonsense look about him, "Have you eaten yet?"

"No," I responded. "I just got off the train from London."

"God!" someone muttered in disgust. "Look what London sends us!"

"Shut up," the boatswain scolded him. Looking at me, he said, "Sit down and eat something."

"Yes, sir," I answered as I dropped my bag to the floor and found an empty swivel chair around the table. "My name's Yurek Iwaszkiewicz," I said, introducing myself to the fellow next to me.

"What ship you from?" he inquired.

"This is my first ship," I answered honestly, and then realized the other men were all listening to our conversation. Trying to make a bid for their approval, I added, "However, I was on the M/S *Chrobry* as an ensign in the Marine Academy." The moment I said this I knew I'd goofed. I never should have mentioned my connection with officers' school. They all clammed up and ignored me.

I was given a cabin to share with Andy the Scot. He was a tall, wiry young man in his late 20s, polite but not very communicative. Of course, he spoke no Polish. After supper he changed his clothes and went ashore. I emptied the contents of my bag into the available closet, washed up and lay on my bunkbed, trying to fall asleep. But sleep wouldn't come. Instead, I felt the old nagging feelings of inadequacy. I was back again at square one, vying for acceptance.

What was it about me that had turned my companions off? Was I too serious about myself? Did I give the impression of being a sissy? Was it my rather cultured command of the Polish language that they disdained? On a ship like this, there was no room or time for niceties. It was a rough crowd, and one had to prove himself to gain the respect of the crew. I'll have to do that, I thought. And then I got angry. After all I'd been through, I asked myself, do I still have to win over these bastards to gain their respect? Then another feeling took hold. I knew that I now had respect for myself. Nobody could take that away from me. Repeating that over and over again to myself, I relaxed and was finally able to fall asleep.

The night watchman woke us the next morning. After breakfast I found the boatswain, who distributed the work detail among the deck crew. "Here," he said, avoiding calling me by my name. "Take this hammer and brush and start chipping the rust off the supports of the harborside raft slides. Be careful how you step so you don't fall off."

Thank God I knew where harborside was, and I climbed up high on the raft. There was barely enough room to wedge in my foot. Soon I was hanging over the ship's gunwhale like a spider. Way down below I saw my reflection in the water. It was cold out there, and the penetrating wind didn't make things any easier. Between trying to keep my balance and chipping away at the rust, I was totally absorbed in my work. After a while, the lunch bell rang.

In the messroom the men wouldn't talk to me. If I started a conversation, they replied in monosyllables. I felt lonely, but I knew it couldn't last forever. Sooner or later, I told myself, I would be accepted by them.

In the meantime, there was a lot to learn. I barely knew the seaman's trade. I watched carefully and learned fast. They still didn't call me by my name. They addressed me as "hey, you."

In Glasgow we had picked up a load of teak that had come all the way from India. Eventually, we set out for Newcastle. Steaming south, we joined several other ships and became part of a convoy. As we approached the English Channel, everyone tensed. These were dangerous waters, infested with German submarines.

The *Krosno*, like most merchant ships, was equipped with two anti-aircraft machine-gun nests and a heavy gun mounted on the aft, serviced by the British Navy gunners. It was January 1944. We steamed in convoy. The cold wind whined as the deck crew performed its various tasks. I learned how to splice a steel cable so it would be capable of pulling the weight of the whole ship. I learned how to sew the canvas hold covers. Despite the rain, which prevented us from painting the ship outside, there was always plenty of work to be done. In foul weather we painted the interior of the ship. The boatswain never ran out of projects to keep us busy.

I envied the wheelhouse watch. They worked in pairs, starting with the so-called captain's watch from 8 p.m. to midnight. The men would return again after eight hours' rest. The man at the wheel, and the lookout watch, alternated every hour. I wished I could steer the ship, and I knew one day I would.

In the meantime, we entered the Channel. No lights were allowed, not even a lit cigarette. Any door to the outside automatically switched off lights if opened. It was a cold, black winter night as I climbed the upper deck to say hello to the radio operator, who was friendly to me. The ships moved closely, one after another. We followed the float pulled by our predecessor. Behind us a Dutch ship followed our float. Suddenly as I looked at our aft I saw a tremendous flash, followed by a deafening explosion. "The Dutchman got it!" the radio operator yelled. We could see the Dutch ship sinking in a blaze of fire. With the distance between us rapidly growing, we heard other explosions. "There goes the engine room!" someone shouted as we watched her slip swiftly under the surface of the water. Everyone gasped, but our ship continued on. Our eyes probed the darkness of the night, trying to detect the German U-boat. In the morning we saw that the Dutchman's place had been taken by a British freighter.

    The next day we changed our course to the north. We were out of the English Channel, and a day later we entered Newcastle Harbor. In the evening everyone got ready to go ashore. I had noticed how the men removed paint from their hands and faces. They took a scoop of butter and some sugar from the kitchen pantry. This made a perfect paint remover, and it never irritated the skin. I followed suit, took a shower, dressed and went into town. I decided to see a movie. I could have tried to join the crew at a nearby bar, but I didn't care for drinking. Besides, I was pretty sure some of the guys would try to pick a fight with me when they were sufficiently drunk. I was already asleep in my cabin when they came back, half-conscious, raising the devil, singing and cursing.

LEFT IN THE COLD

The next day I was lowered overboard on a boatswain's chair to chip rust. The boatswain's chair is simply a short piece of board on which one sits as on a swing. The ropes on either end can be manipulated by the sitter to lower the seat by a gravity-controlled slip knot. No one could see me there, because I was on the basin side.

It was a very cold winter day and I was pummelled by nasty gusts of a penetrating wind. Well, I thought, consoling myself, another couple of hours of this and I'll thaw out in the messroom at lunch. I kept chipping away at the rust. I was so tightly wedged into the seat I could hardly move. Beneath me, reflected in the water, I saw the soles of my shoes.

I looked at my wristwatch. It was getting close to the noon lunch break. I was feeling stiff from the cold. I

ESCAPE INTO DANGER

banged my feet against the steel hull, trying to warm them. Someone will be coming any minute now, I thought, to pull me up for lunch. I heard the bell ring 12 noon. They were late. I started to worry. Could it be they had forgotten me? I couldn't be seen there, so I shouted: "Hey, up on deck, anyone!" But no one answered. Only the seagulls responded, laughing at me in their unique way. I shouted again. It was getting close to one o'clock. I tried to warm myself, but being so immobilized made it very difficult. I watched the hours go by, and I shouted till my throat was sore. After a while, I could barely get out a sound.

It was well after 5 p.m. when the boatswain, checking out the progress of work, finally noticed the ropes securing my weight. He leaned over the rail, saw me and let out a string of curses. "*Anyone! Here! On the double!*" he shouted. I heard several men running. "Who was the sonofabitch who left this guy hanging all day?" the boatswain yelled. They pulled me in. I was so numb I could barely stand.

"How about some overtime pay?" I croaked to the boatswain in my raspy voice. "I've been sitting here since eight this morning." Then I saw the man who had lowered me down. He was the same one who had made nasty remarks on that first day, when I introduced myself. I walked over to him and, before he realized what was happening, I punched him with all my strength. He fell back, tripping over a coil of rope. With a curse, he got up and threw himself at me. I managed to give him a black eye before the boatswain restrained both of us. "O.K., that's enough," he yelled. "Now I don't want to hear anymore about it."

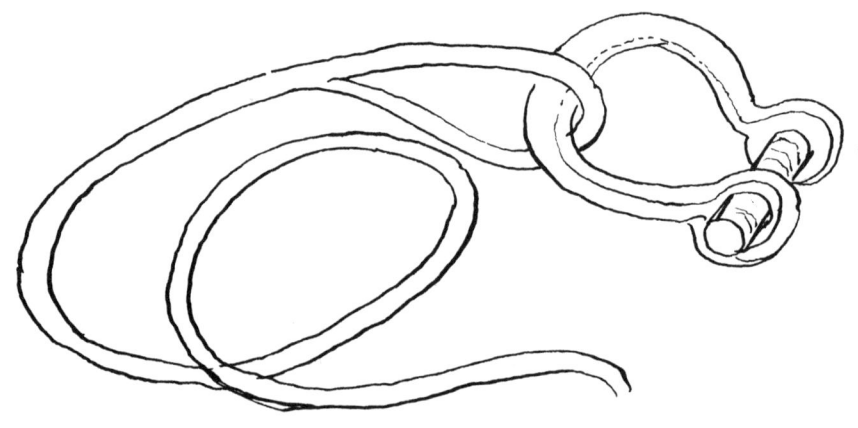

ACCEPTANCE

When we left Newcastle, loaded with new cargo, we went north along the east coast of England. In the following months, the *Krosno* made several runs around England, and I learned a lot about seamanship.

One day we came back to Newcastle. That's when the crew finally accepted me and started calling me by my first name. It happened this way. One morning during the loading of a special cache of military cargo, a steel cable slipped and a shackle at its eye end wedged itself in the upper tip of a stationary derrick. There was no way to free the shackle. Underneath the derrick stood the boatswain and several of the men, looking up and debating various ways to solve the problem. A few things were tried, but nothing worked. There was a steel cable supporting the

ACCEPTANCE

derrick. If someone could climb the cable, he could free the shackle. But that was unlikely, since the cable dripped with grease.

That's when I said to the boatswain, "I can climb up there."

He looked at me impatiently and said, "Don't talk nonsense. It's too slippery."

"I know I can do it," I insisted. "Let me try."

"All right," he said, reluctantly, shaking his head.

I went to the storeroom and got some rags and a can of kerosene. I soaked the rags in the kerosene and hooked them to my belt. Then I put on leather gloves and began to climb.

Even as a child I had always been a good climber. There hadn't been a tree I couldn't master. As I moved up, I wrapped my legs tightly around the cable and pulled myself up by my arms. I must have looked like a giant insect inching my way up and up. When I saw patches of grease, I hung on with one hand and pulled out a kerosene-soaked rag with the other, wiping the area. The kerosene cut the grease, and I had enough friction to assist my climb. I was quite high up when I slipped down about a yard, but I managed to grasp rags with both hands and steady myself. Below me the men stood watching. I didn't dare look down. Another yard and another superhuman effort, and I was grasping the derrick. Then I pulled on the shackle and dislodged it. It went down by its own weight, pulling the lead cable with it. The men grabbed it, cheering for me. From where I was, looking down, they seemed very small.

I took a deep breath and slowly let myself down. I felt my gloves burn just as I hit the deck. They were smoking when I pulled them off. The boatswain came over to me, shook my hand and said, "I'll be damned! Good job, Yurek!"

THE WHEEL AND THE COMPASS

Through the spring of 1945 we ran various errands delivering military equipment. The ships in the English Channel were crowded together like sardines in a can. Our next run was to the north. Since that gave us more room to move about, I asked the boatswain to let me learn steering. With the approval of the second officer, I reported to the wheelhouse. After some instruction, I was allowed to lay my hands on the wheel. It seemed easy, but I found myself turning the wheel from one end to the other, not able to stay on course. Captain Mikszta came running out of the chart room and demanded to know what was going on.

"A seaman in training, sir," answered the second officer.

"Grab the wheel for a moment," the captain told him. Then he asked me to walk outside with him and pointed out the zigzag pattern of the ship's wake. "You have to be patient with the wheel," he told me. "Look at the compass and let the needle move slowly. The ship is heavy. She takes her time to turn before she gets on course. Give her a bit of a counter turn. That will stabilize her."

"I understand, sir," I said. "I'll do my best." I took the wheel from the second officer. He said the course number and I repeated it loudly.

I learned quickly, and in a few days I was able to stay on course quite well. So I asked the boatswain for a wheelwatch assignment. Much to my surprise and delight, I was given the eight-to-midnight watch with Andy. "You're lucky," the boatswain told me. "You're taking the place of Stanley, who's going to the hospital." That's how I became not only a helmsman, but later a *maneuvering* helmsman—a special distinction for accuracy in steering, which is necessary in difficult approaches to harbors and in working with a pilot's instructions. I could now steer the ship as if it were my own car.

Many trips later, the *Krosno* again steamed north along the east coast of England. On a beautiful dark night in May, with the air smelling of salty seaweed, I was at the wheel and Andy was on lookout outside. It was so quiet in the wheelhouse one could hear the ticking of the clock. I had my eyes on the floating compass, which swayed slightly in the gentle sea swells and glowed with a soft green light.

All of a sudden Captain Mikszta seemed to be excited about something. He ran outside and peered into the night with his binoculars. He cursed softly and called the first officer on the ship's phone. "I know we should see a red signal from a coast buoy here, but I don't see anything," he said. The captain ran back and forth, looking out again. Then Andy burst in, shouting, "Land on course!" Just then the captain ordered, "Starboard hard!" and pulled the lever to STOP on the engine telegraph. Suddenly we hit bottom.

THE WHEEL AND THE COMPASS

Everybody and everything loose flew forward. I felt my ribs smash against the steering wheel. "Full astern!" the captain shouted and turned the telegraph handle down. We heard the ship's propeller turning wildly, going nowhere. We were grounded. The captain let out a string of curses. "Radio, call shore," he ordered. "Buoy No. 24 is out!"

I was still holding the wheel. "Check the high-tide timetable," the captain called. We were in the middle of an outgoing tide, and by dawn the *Krosno* listed slowly to one side. "Don't worry, men," the captain said, speaking through a bullhorn. "We're reaching the bottom of low tide. She'll list even more. We're waiting for high tide to get us off."

I went to my cabin and put all my papers in a plastic bag. The ship listed so much it was difficult to walk. Finally the sun broke through and I saw a tugboat offering us a thick manila rope. One of the crew grabbed it and hooked it up. Quickly the tugboat lurched backward, tightening the rope like a piano string. "Get that rope off!" screamed the captain. "Get it off!" The boatswain ran over, shouting at the tugboatman to loosen up, but he held tight. Then the boatswain ran off and returned with an ax. "Loosen up," he shouted, "or I'll cut you off." With that the tugboat moved closer and we threw his rope overboard. "You'll be sorry," the man yelled, pointing to the sea behind us. We turned around and saw two magnetic mines only a few hundred yards away. "Gunners on action station!" roared Mikszta. He ran to his cabin and came back with a high-powered rifle. The British gunners were ready within a minute and were told to shoot the mines. We watched in awe as the heavy gun recoiled in a deafening explosion. They missed by far. The captain aimed and fired five times in a row. Suddenly one of the mines exploded in a great fountain of water. The gunners finally got the other one. That night the high tide freed us from the shallows. We backed up and were on course again.

END OF THE WAR!

It was August 1945. We steamed along the shore around the outermost parts of Scotland. Then one day we were told there was an unexpected change of plans. We were to enter a quiet bay surrounded by craggy mountains. The bay had no harbor or any signs of human habitation. However, we noticed that several other ships were anchored there. In few moments we, too, dropped anchor. "All hands on deck" came the order from the bridge. Hastily, we assembled. The captain turned toward us, smiling, a bullhorn to his lips. "Men," he said, "I have very good news to tell you. Germany has surrendered. The war is over! Today we will all celebrate. Long live peace!"

Everyone screamed, "Hip, hip, hurrah!"

We heard shouting and singing from the other ships

END OF THE WAR!

as well. The crews were dressing their vessels in a great gala. A great gala is a long line of flags tied from the bow through the tops of both masts. "I need a volunteer to go up and hang our gala," the boatswain shouted.

"I'll go, " I yelled back.

It started to rain as I began to climb the aft mast. The metal ladder became narrower and narrower the higher I climbed. When I was about 10 feet from the top, a metal rung broke under my foot and I began to fall. I flailed my arms and caught a lower step. Then I looked down, and my heart started pounding. I was so high up, the deck looked miniscule. I thought if I dropped a coin it would surely fall into the sea. The men were so small I couldn't even hear their voices. Well, I won't look down, I told myself, and I resumed climbing.

When I reached the broken rung again, I looked it over. It was rust-eaten. It must have been a long time since anyone had been up there. From then on, I tried every step carefully before putting any weight on it. When I finally got to the top, I held onto the apple of the mast, pulling my line through the swivel block and letting it go down. I marveled at the view from up there. Then, in a few moments, I was down. The men pulled on the line and hoisted all the flags to the top.

Oh, how difficult it was for me to comprehend that the war was finally over. I never doubted that the Nazis would be defeated. It was only a matter of time. But when that time actually came, I was so well armored with the defenses necessary for survival that several hours passed before I finally allowed any emotion to surface. Even then, everything seemed unreal, and I had great difficulty accepting the long-awaited fulfillment of my dreams. For six long years I had to count the hours, the days, the weeks, the months, each time ending in disappointment.

The incomprehensibleness of this situation was further compounded by the strange, surrealistic setting I found myself in. When we anchored, this quiet bay had seemed unreal, surrounded by mountains reminiscent of a lunar landscape, and all was deathly still. Only the occasional eerie laughter of a passing seagull broke the silence. Then, suddenly, as if by magic, the whole bay took on the appearance of an operatic stage set. Many ships appeared, each bedecked with multicolored ornaments and festive lights. The sounds of cheering and music and hearty celebration drifted over this strange scene. I felt disoriented and alone, as if I were somewhere at the ends of the earth, still clinging to my last shreds of hope, unable to fully comprehend that my dreams had finally come true.

I realized that events would swiftly follow one after another, and soon I'd see my family and friends again. But I didn't dwell on that. Mostly my mind was filled with the painful memories of those long years I had lived through. Even though the Nazi monster was finally slain, it had left death and destruction in its wake. I knew that my recurring nightmares would haunt me forever. I'll have to come to terms with them, I thought. Perhaps someday I'll write a book, I told myself, or make paintings about what I saw and felt.

In the meantime, the crew of the *Krosno* was celebrating. There was a lot of whiskey and food, singing and cheering. It wasn't until noon the next day that the crew sobered up enough to get the ship going. Two days later we docked in Liverpool.

SHIPLESS IN LONDON

With the end of the war, new political problems presented themselves to me. The press and radio reports indicated that, despite its liberation, Poland was not free at all. The Soviet Red Army was cruelly enforcing Stalin's rule. The present Polish government consisted of Moscow-trained Polish politicians. All Polish refugees returning to Poland were considered to have been infected with capitalism and were undesirable to the new regime. Many who returned reported mistreatment. In view of this, a number of my fellow seamen decided to follow a policy of "wait and see." Consequently, they left their ships and stayed temporarily in London. I was caught up in the whirlpool of these events and left the *Krosno* with the rest of the crew. This was considered a furlough, and the shipping company paid us a meager temporary subsistence.

London was not new to me; I had no difficulty finding a room. I wondered how my family in Poland was—hoping they had survived the war, hoping they had received my mail. I couldn't call them, because I didn't know where they were.

It was the summer of 1945. I was 23. I visited an outstanding exhibition of photographs depicting the horrors of war. One pavilion was dedicated to the war with Japan. I saw photos of life-size soldiers lurking in jungle thickets. I heard the sounds of birds in the tropical forests. The giant photos imparted a sense of reality, danger and fear of death. Another pavilion showed the Nazi atrocities in Europe. Incredible as it seems to me now, that was the first time I heard of the mass extermination of Jews in German concentration camps. Large photos showed thousands of corpses in uncovered mass graves, the ovens of Auschwitz and the emaciated faces and bodies of the survivors. I read the descriptions of these events, and my head spinned in horror. Catholic Poles as well as Jews had died in concentration camps. Poles were hated by the Germans, and the Jews even more so. To make things worse, many Poles also despised the Jews. It was easy to cultivate anti-Semitism in Poland.

SOMETHING IN COMMON

There are many ways one learns to love or to hate. Some say those feelings are acquired with the mother's milk. In Poland it was easy to learn to hate the Jews, because they were so different. They kept to themselves with their own customs, language and religious rituals. They were considered strangers, because they didn't share in the national patriotism. Rather, they had their eyes and hearts on Jerusalem. That's how the Catholic Poles felt about the Polish Jews. The Jews were also considered to be both rich capitalists and rebellious Communists. Paradoxically, they were blamed for both ideologies, despite the logical and obvious inconsistencies. But prejudice does not know logic. Instead it thrives on the need to find a scapegoat to blame for the misery and despair of one's daily life.

The Jews were such a scapegoat. Ukrainians and

Protestants were also undesirables in Poland, because not being Catholic meant that one was not a true Pole.

I recall that there were no Jewish families in my little village of Bogdanovo, and only a few in that western part of Poland near Poznan. I also remember derogatory expressions regarding Jews. These expressions were permanently embedded in the everyday language. For instance, the splash of black ink that often stained a school child's homework was called a "Jew," while its real name is *kleks*. Thus, as a child, without ever having seen any Jews, I already felt they were undesirable people. It could have been very easy for me to become a Jew hater, but I was very fortunate. My parents did not allow such prejudice in our home. Besides, my mother had grown up in the predominantly Jewish town of Grojec, near Warsaw, and had enjoyed the mutual respect and friendship of her Jewish neighbors. Eventually there came a time when my parents felt I should leave our village to discover wider horizons. When I was ready for junior high school, I was sent to live with my uncle's family in the large town of Gdynia. That's where I met my first Jew.

His name was Hal Kulig. Hal was a rather small boy for his age and not very athletic. Since I wasn't very athletic either, we had something in common. Also, we were both disliked by the tough clique that ruled our class, and that was one of the reasons we became friends. The other was that I was failing algebra, and Hal, being a good student, often helped me with it.

A bully named Stanley Pietrovski used to push us both around. I will never forget his name, because Stanley caused me a lot of grief and provoked me into a fight. I spent long hours daydreaming of revenge. But Stanley was a good boxer and bigger than all of us.

Finally, I convinced myself that I couldn't live with his humiliation anymore. I decided that the next time he provoked me I'd accept the challenge and hit him with all my might. I knew there was a possibility that I could hurt him. After classes I often spent time with Hal, and I told him of my plan. He tried to talk me out of it, but I had made up my mind. I knew the element of surprise would work in my favor. If I were able to score a couple of good punches, I'd be happy. That was all I could really hope for, since Stanley could overpower me with sheer weight alone. No matter what he did, though, I knew I'd live through it.

One day I asked Hal, "Why do they pick on me?"

"They wouldn't if you'd look tougher," he said, "and besides, your voice is gentle, like a girl's." He sighed. "And they pick on me because I'm a Jew."

I knew I had a thin voice, but to be thought of as sounding like a girl made me angry enough to fight anyone. "And they hate you because you're a Jew?" I asked, a questioning note in my voice. "Then why don't you change to our religion? Then you'd have no more problems."

Hal, obviously hurt, looked at me and said, "My religion is a personal thing, and that doesn't make anyone good or bad."

"But doesn't it make you angry to be so disliked?" I asked. "Don't you want to punch someone in the nose?"

"I'd like to, but I'm not allowed to," Hal replied. "My parents told me never to fight, because that would make them hate me even more. Besides," he added, "I'm not an athlete like Stanley. He'd kill me."

I knew exactly what to do. The day of reckoning had come. One sunny spring morning Hal and I were playing ball and fooling around during recess. Stanley, along with a few of his cohorts, walked over and pushed me, saying mockingly, "And how is my sweetheart today?" Everyone laughed.

"Much better than yesterday," I answered and punched him hard, following that up with a couple of quick jabs to the face. Stanley was taken by surprise, and for a few seconds I scored. Then he lunged at me with all his weight, punching me furiously all over my face. I changed from attack to defense, covering my head with both hands. That's when the bell rang, signaling the end of recess, and the fight was over. My face burned, and in some places it was numb, like wood. I could barely see through my swollen eyelids, but what I saw was enough to make me feel good. Stanley was growing a beautiful black eye.

    That evening, when I went to Hal's house for help with my algebra, I learned his mother had baked some poppyseed strudel . . . just for me.

THE LETTER

As I looked at the Holocaust photos, I thought of Hal. Had he managed to escape and save his life? Had my family survived the war? As I asked myself those questions, I didn't yet know that, at that very moment, a letter with the answer about my family was on its way to me.

During my stay in London I frequently visited the National Gallery, studying the paintings of Old Masters. Then I'd go to my rented room and work on drawings and watercolors. This gave me a lot of pleasure, and I spent a good deal of time indoors, sketching the scenes I saw from my window. I thought often about my family and missed them very much. So far the inquiries I made at the Red Cross had not produced any information.

One day I received a notice from my shipping company that I was to pick up my documents and join the crew of the S/S *Bialystok* in Liverpool. The next day I packed my bag and reported to the company office, where I received my papers and instructions. There was also a letter for me. I quickly pocketed it, as I had to rush to catch the Liverpool train. I just made it. Racing for the door of the departing train, I jumped in, pulled my bag in after me, and, exhausted, collapsed on a seat. The train started to move noiselessly, and soon under my feet I felt the rhythmic motion and clicking of the iron wheels.

I was just about to doze off when I became aware of a nagging thought knocking on the door of my mind. What have I forgotten? I asked myself. And then I remembered the letter. Quickly I took it out of my pocket and looked at it. It had British post stamps on it and was from my Uncle Klim, who, according to his return address, had also been in London. I ripped the envelope open and started to read. My uncle informed me that my family had survived the war, all except my sister Viesia. She had died shortly before the war ended.

I was stunned. She meant so much to me. I had so looked forward to seeing her again. How could fate be so cruel? No! I just could not accept it. I folded the letter, slipped it in the envelope and put it back in my pocket. I refused to think about what I'd just learned for a long time—not until I heard about it again from my parents' own lips.

S/S BIALYSTOK

The crew of the *Bialystok* was a strange mixture of nationalities and characters. Many of them were vagabonds, often referred to as the scum of the earth. Some were smugglers, knifers or fugitives from justice. The *Bialystok* was a tramp ship in its full meaning. Like a gypsy, she never knew where tomorrow would bring her. And like a true tramp, she roamed all over the world for profit. No one knew if she would some day steam for Poland. She was a large ship of the Liberty class, coal fed and therefore dirty. In fact, dirty was my first impression of her.

As I descended the iron steps leading to the crew's cabins, I saw a drunken brawl. One of the seamen was beating another senseless. I didn't intend to interfere until I saw that the victim was bleeding profusely and not resisting. The attacker banged his opponent's head against the iron deck. I thought he'd never stop. He was killing the man!

"Cut it out!" I yelled, grabbing the seaman's shoulders from behind. He wrestled with me, but I managed to restrain him. By then I was no pushover but a seasoned seaman. Besides, the man was drunk and I was sober. This gave the victim a chance to get up and get away. As he did, he left behind a trail of blood. I let go of the attacker, who by now was cursing me. But he didn't try to follow me as I proceeded to look for my cabin. When I found it, I wasn't happy to learn that he was one of my three bunkmates.

"Maday is his name," said a young Polish fellow who occupied the bunk below mine. "He's a troublemaker." Then he added, "My name's Pavel. I only joined this crew a few weeks ago, and already I've seen him in a fight a couple of times. He's a heavy drinker."

"Well, I'll stay out of his way as much as I can, but I sure didn't like to see the other guy getting slaughtered," I said as I put away the contents of my bag.

Pavel was about my age. He looked at me with an ever-present little smile, behind which the real Pavel hid. In fact, the real Pavel was so well hidden behind his seemingly innocent blue eyes that it took me quite a while to realize he was almost as nasty a fellow as Maday.

The fourth occupant of our cabin showed up later. Everybody called him *Ukrainietz*, which in Polish means "Ukrainian." He gave the impression of being a hard, sadistic individual. He had a taciturn face, with high Mongolian cheekbones and cold gray eyes that emitted an impudent stare, immediately discouraging any eye contact. Strands of blond hair sneaked out from under his greasy black fisherman's cap, which was a permanent fixture atop his head. He even slept with it on. Ukrainietz spoke slowly, in an eastern Polish drawl. Also, slowly but steadily, he drank vodka in large quantities, which made him and Maday pals.

It is interesting how the nicknames of various individuals get coined. The crew didn't abound in creative intelligence and didn't seem to work very hard in naming their shipmates. For example, they called a giant Yugoslavian *Yugoslav* and a Rumanian *Ruman*. An Arab, whose job was feeding the coal furnaces in the ship's belly, was called *L'Arbie*. A man who worked with L'Arbie, a tall, dark, handsome Spaniard, was called *Fernando* and was known for his romances in every port. Women were crazy about him, and everyone on the *Bialystok* envied Fernando his amorous successes. There was also an older, gray-haired seaman called *Stary,* which in Polish means "the old one." Stary was very quiet and never drank. Instead, he read books. Despite these profound differences that separated him from the others, Stary enjoyed the respect of the crew because he was an experienced seaman. I struck up a friendship with him and also with Yugoslav. Yugoslav was a gentle giant. Though he spoke only Serbo-Croatian, I could understand him. He was a very powerful man with hands as large as frying pans. I felt lucky to get the 4-to-8-a.m. watch with him. Our boatswain, Levicki, was a rather innocuous man of medium build who knew his trade well. Otherwise, there wasn't anything particularly interesting about him.

At that time we were on our way to Newfoundland to pick up iron ore for England's steel mills. I liked steering the ship. She was much larger than the *Krosno,* but, since she was empty, she was very sensitive to every touch of the wheel. I stood behind it, my feet slightly apart, planted firmly on the perforated wooden mat board, my hands lightly on the wheel spokes, my eyes fixed on the needle of the gently swaying face of the compass. At times I shifted my eyes to see the ship's bow rise and fall rhythmically. I heard the gentle ticking of the clock, which showed 6 a.m. Presently the door to the bridge wing opened and Yugoslav came to relieve me. "Three, one, two," I said, giving him the course. "Three, one, two," he repeated. I pulled on my oilskin and went out on the bridge wing.

The night was lit by a full moon, which soon revealed itself from behind some silver-edged clouds. The moonlight sparkled on the shifting swells and made a silver sea path toward the far horizon. A cold December wind blew on my face, but I felt good. I had one hour of lookout before relieving Yugoslav. Staying alert didn't prevent me from enjoying my solitude. This was a marvelous place to be, to feel the magnificent serenity of the sea and sky and yet also to be on the move toward new horizons. I dreamed many dream-thoughts on nights like that, when one could contemplate the vastness of the universe reflected in a million sparkling stars. The sheer fragility of my existence there, wedged between the endlessness of space and the vastness of the ocean, highlighted not only my humble limitations but also my insolent daring for adventure. That's what life is for me, good or bad, I realized. As long as I can breathe, it will always be an adventure. I still find it difficult to imagine boredom, because no two moments in life are the same. I always find life rich by the mere act of living.

MALTED

At seven I relieved Yugoslav at the wheel. The grayness of a gloomy dawn made its slow way into morning. Yugoslav went down to wake up the day crew for the next watch. At eight Maday took my place and Ukrainietz relieved Yugoslav. I walked to the messroom, inhaling the strong smells of coffee and of ham and eggs. I had six hours to myself. After breakfast, I went to sleep in my cabin.

The rocking motion of the ship woke me. I realized we were running into foul weather. Indeed, when I went outside, I saw that the sun had gone behind dark gray clouds. The wind blew steadily, and the waves grew bigger and wilder. Bad weather in the North Atlantic during winter is quite common, and it offered no exception for us. When land finally appeared, everyone felt better.

We didn't have shore leave at Bell Isle, where we

took on our cargo of iron ore. It was the fastest loading operation I had ever witnessed. Our holds were filled in a few hours, as easily as one fills a sugar bowl from a spouted bag.

Our next stop was St. John's, Nova Scotia, where we were allowed to go ashore. That was my first contact with the opulence of North America. I went into town with Stary and was amazed to see so many stores and the variety of goods displayed in their windows, all gleaming with Christmas decorations. We stopped at a milk bar and sat down at the counter. At Stary's suggestion, I ordered an ice-cream malted. I'd never had one before. I liked it so much I tried every flavor they had. The rest of the crew had gone to the nearest bar. They came back drunk and were badly hung over the next day. As for me, the next day I concluded that it was still better to get sick from an overdose of malteds than of alcohol.

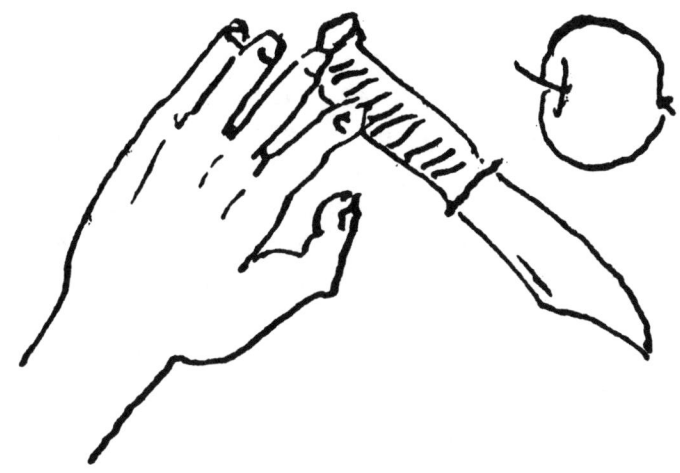

FIGHT

In the messroom at lunchtime, Maday started to bait me. I knew he hated me, both because I had restrained him my first day on board and because I didn't drink.

"So you think you're better than the rest of us, you chickenshit!" he sneered, trying to provoke me. He was peeling an apple with his hunting knife.

"Watch your language," I admonished him. With that, he dropped the apple and lunged at me with the knife. I was anticipating that reaction, so I ducked as his hand with the knife shot past my neck. Then I grabbed his hand with both of mine and twisted and jerked it. The knife fell to the floor. Immediately we were both out of our chairs and wrestling. We fell to the floor, and soon Maday was on top of me, banging my head on the deck. He was getting the better of me. In a flash I recalled the scene of him doing the same thing to the other fellow. I'll never allow him to do that to me, I thought, and my anger gave me such a jolt of strength that I twisted out from under his weight, hooked my leg between his and, using his weight as leverage, swiftly straightened out and got on top of him. Then I grabbed him by the hair and banged *his* head on the deck. I felt such a surge of energy that I dominated him completely. But at that point Ukrainietz started to kick me in the kidneys. The next thing I knew, Yugoslav was yelling. He grabbed Ukrainietz by the neck and flung him against the wall.

In a moment my anger was gone. I'd had enough. I didn't feel like punishing Maday anymore. It was obvious that I had won the fight. I stood up and extended my hand to him. "Let's shake and forget about it," I said.

But he pushed my hand away. "I'll get you for this!" he spat, and stormed out. I picked up his knife, followed him and . . . threw the knife overboard.

TEMPEST

We left St. John's in a gathering storm, which in the next few hours grew into a full-blown gale. When I took the wheel at 4 a.m., the wind was so strong that it amassed wave after wave into towering mountains of water. The ship was tossed in those steep slopes and deep valleys like a child's toy. Half the time steering proved ineffectual. I saw the ship veer off course by 45 degrees in a single moment. Then she would turn as much the other way.

    The captain and the third officer stood by, watchful. As the ship was tossed to the top of a huge wave, she poised for a moment, then crashed down into the opening abyss, diving like a whale, bow first. The propeller, no longer submerged, went into a loud and violent spin that made the ship vibrate almost to the point of exploding. I watched her plunge so deep that the whole foredeck was under the foaming brine. Everything loose slid forward, and I was pinned to the wheel. With silent prayers on our lips, we counted long seconds.

Then, slowly, she rose, spilling off gallons of white water on both sides. The same wave that had kept her down then started to rise, more and more, till the ship paused like a diver on the edge of a board poised for the next leap. I held my breath as she plunged again, slamming deep into the black sea, which closed completely over the whole deck. Then she was pinned down by another gigantic mass of water, which quickly rose up like a mountain and crashed against her starboard side with such vehemence that it smashed the door to the wheelhouse, drenching all of us with brine. Burdened with the second wave, she stayed down for quite a while, and I thought, That's it. We're done for! But then she slowly emerged, like a whale coming up for air, spewing the foaming sea all over. Like a sharp knife, the force of the water had cut the iron rails supporting the life raft, which was now gone, and only twisted steel jutted out into the fury of the night, like clawing fingers in the agony of death. "Starboard hard!" yelled the captain. "We must have her face the wind!"

"Starboard hard!" I responded. She began to turn slowly, hesitatingly. Then he snapped, "Midships, steady as she goes."

"Midships, steady as she goes," I echoed.

At 5 a.m. Yugoslav took the wheel and I put on a hooded storm coat and went outside. The smashed door still hung limply on partially twisted hinges. The wind howled like a hundred demons in Hell. I could see the towering mountains of blackish-blue water slamming and sweeping over us. The sky was an ominous gray, and the lead-colored clouds hung low, chased by gusts of cold wind.

I was sent aft to bring the log readings and was almost swept overboard by a big wave. As I saw it coming,

I grasped the guard rail with both hands and took a deep breath. But the onrushing water struck with such force that it opened my hands and threw me against the entrance to the crew's quarters, where I lay for a moment, bruised and choking.

Finally, the sea calmed. I went in to alert the next watch. It had been impossible for the men to sleep while being tossed so violently from side to side. When I went outside again I noticed two arctic owls resting on the gunwale rails. Those large, magnificent birds had simply been blown out of the Newfoundland forest by the storm and were lucky to have found the ship to rest on. They stayed with us all the way to Liverpool and then left, probably for the cold north region of Scotland. We licked our wounds as the storm abated. Ruman broke his arm as he was hit by a crushing wave. Almost everyone paid some tribute to the fury of Neptune.

I was at the wheel as we entered Belfast, Ireland. I tried to be very accurate, since I was building a reputation as a talented maneuvering helmsman.

Christmas 1945 came the next day. We celebrated in our messroom, whose walls we decorated with flags. We ate and drank and sang Polish songs. That's when Maday came over to me with a bottle of vodka, and, after having a couple of swigs together, we shook hands.

CHRISTMAS

Christmas always reminds me of home and still fills my heart with fond memories. As far as I am concerned, it has little to do with God and religion, even if it is supposed to be God's birthday. I am not a believer, yet the spirit of Christmas is still special in my memories. I don't know why we wait until Christmas with our charity for the needy. Why save our morality for that particular day? As I write this, I feel old and heavy with so many experiences. But I think my soul is still tender, and my feelings grow ever deeper. In many ways, I am still an innocent. I can cry without shame and laugh without feeling silly about it. So when I say I like to remember my Christmases at home when I was a child, it means I am weaving a sentimental tale. On a cold, December day, when I inhale the aroma of evergreens, I just

CHRISTMAS

shut my eyes and push my memory button.

There I see myself as a small child. It is Christmas Eve. The kitchen is full of exciting smells. Everyone exudes an air of mystery. Adults are talking in riddles and there is the expectation of great surprises to come. It is snowing outside. Soon devils and angels will knock at our door. But not yet.

Our father is nowhere to be found. The door to the living room is closed. My sisters, Marysia and Ania, stand waiting in front of it. So do my mother and I.

A husky voice, the husky voice of the master, calls from behind the door. A "Santa" follows. We children answer a question or two about arithmetic, history, geography. Then we each have to recite a poem. We all get words of praise from "Santa." Finally, we hear the stomping of heavy footsteps departing.

Suddenly our father is with us again and he says, "Why don't we open the door?" I excitedly try to explain to him that Santa was just here in a great, secret appearance and doesn't want anyone to see him. But father bravely opens the door anyway. There before us is a beautiful Christmas tree. It has sparkling tapers and colorful twisted candles glowing in their individual auras of light. Glass balls are reflecting the sparklers and the candles. I see dangling candies wrapped in iridescent foil and shimmering angel hair, and the gay festoons of colored-paper chains. Beneath the aromatic fir branches hide carefully wrapped gifts with little name tags. Each package shows care and love. And each holds the promise of a surprise. I pick up one of mine and shake it to get an inkling of its contents. There are "a-a-ahs" and "o-o-ohs," excitement and joy, and the words ". . . just what I always wanted!" And "thank you, thank you." Then we all go to the dining room, because supper is ready. Our maid is considered part of the family. After she receives her gifts, she serves the food and then joins us at the table under the soft light of the kerosene lamps.

The first course is mushroom soup, made from the dried mushrooms we picked ourselves last summer. Then comes boiled pike in its own jellied juice. The pike is decorated with slices of carrot and is served cold. Then pierogis, stuffed with sauerkraut and mushrooms. Then noodles with kasha, red beets and boiled potatoes with horseradish sauce. Finally chocolate-glazed gingerbread, cookies, nuts and candies. And last, hot tea served in glasses.

After supper we gather again in the living room, and Viesia plays some Chopin etudes and mazurkas on the piano. As I listen to the music, I marvel at the chocolate ornaments hanging from the tree branches on silver and golden threads. There are chocolate iceskates, butterflies, violins and little angels wrapped in gaily printed silver foil. They are both good to look at and good to eat. Later, we all sing carols with mother at the piano and father playing the violin.

Outside the dogs start to bark. We hear the sound of bells and a knocking at the front door. Father opens it and welcomes in a group of performers. There are devils jingling with chains coiled around their necks, angels with wings of white tissue that look like real feathers and a king with a beautiful, gold-painted cardboard crown. They all perform, carefully reciting their parts. Afterward, my father gives them a few coins, which fall with loud clinks into their metal money box. As they leave through the open door, I see snowflakes dancing in the yellow light of the kerosene street lamp, and the whole world looks like a Christmas card . . . .

CHRISTMAS

With Viesia, 1924

Viesia and I

ESCAPE INTO DANGER

With my parents and Viesia

In my velvet suit with Viesia

Our home and schoolhouse

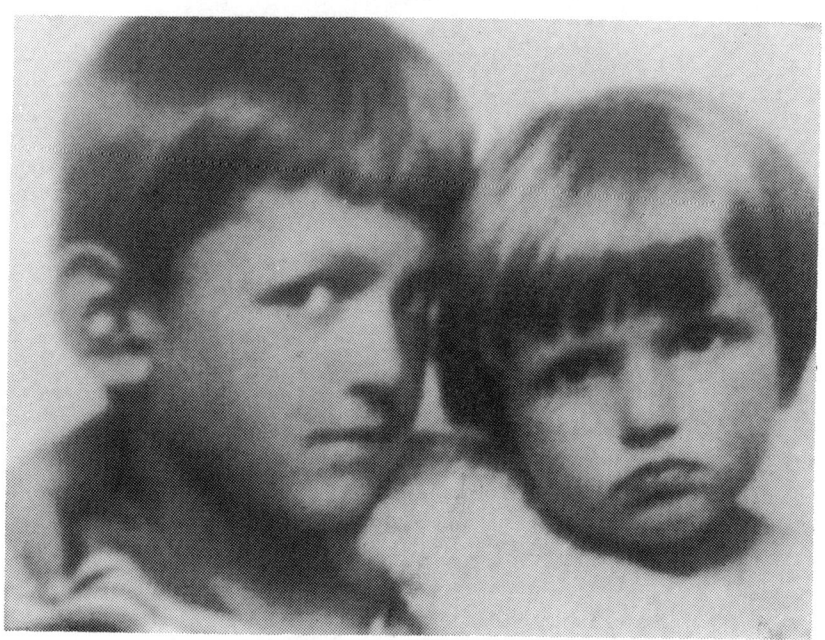
With Marysia, 1929

With my mother, Marysia, my father and Viesia at my parents' 25th anniversary, January 3, 1939, six months before I left for South America

My cousin, my father and I just before leaving for South America, 1939

CHRISTMAS

With shipmates, Winter 1939, London

I'm the one far left in the sailor suit,
leaving with volunteers for France, 1939

ESCAPE INTO DANGER

With a shipmate,
Winter 1939, London

My POW dogtag, Weissenburg,
Germany, 1941

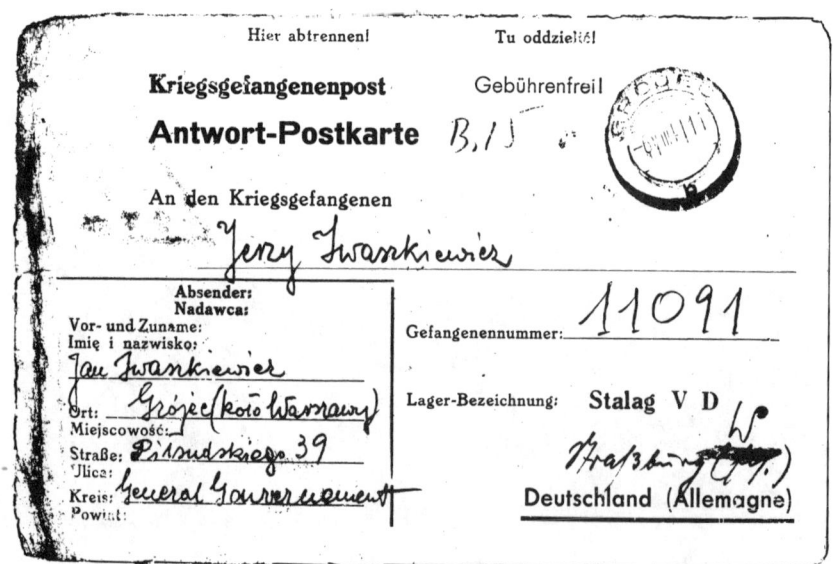

Postcard from my father received in POW camp

CHRISTMAS

Left to right: Franek, I and Tadek in Madrid

L to R: Messboy, Ruman, Yugoslav, Boatswain Levicki, Ukrainietz (*with owl*), L'Arbie and Maday (*with owl*). After tempest at sea

L to R: Unidentified, Maday, Pavel, 3rd officer (*behind Pavel*), I and Ukrainietz (*with his arm around me*). Christmas in Belfast

Two guys and Fernando (*right*) on
Bialystok at sea

S/S *Bialystok*

Maday and arctic owl after tempest
on *Bialystok*

CHRISTMAS

With two guys on *Bialystok*

I'm working at sea

On the *Bialystok*

British destroyer HMS *Antilope*, 1943

Back in England, Polish Army, 1943

Arriving in New York harbor

After bout with pneumonia

CHRISTMAS

My medical discharge from *Bialystok*

Iris and I at my 70th birthday party, Cranbury, NJ, July 5, 1992

RESERVED SEAT

The *Bialystok* made many trips, and one of them was to North Africa. It was early spring 1946 when we docked at Casablanca. Late one afternoon, with chores all squared away, the crew ventured ashore.

I went with Charlie, the ship's cook, who told me he knew his way around the city. As soon as we set foot on land, we were approached by a swarm of vendors and moneychangers. After fending them off, we found ourselves on a cobblestone harbor road fringed with dingy restaurants and small shops. At a small sidewalk cafe we sat down and ordered wine. Presently a young man came over and offered to exchange, very favorably, our English pounds for French francs. Charlie took him up on it and, when the hasty, under-the-table transaction was over, discovered that he had been cheated tenfold, literally. The young fellow had folded the banknotes in such a manner that the zeros were doubled, and thus a ten-franc note appeared to be a hundred to the untrained eye. "Damn it!" Charlie cursed. "That sonofabitch just ripped me off!"

"Don't worry, " I said. "I still have some money on me."

The sun was setting as we strolled deeper into town. Still in the harbor district, we walked in the middle of the street, because the sidewalks were lined with turbanned Moroccans squatting or leaning against the dingy walls. They scrutinized all foreigners with hungry eyes and seemed to be evaluating our clothing, wristwatches and the contents of our pockets. Dirt, squalor and hopeless poverty mixed with hate surrounded us in an almost palpable way. As we passed them, we felt their intense gaze boring into our backs. We knew we were easy prey and felt like sheep among hungry wolves. Our nervous tension hung thick in the air as we hastened our steps.

And then it started. First, some children pulled at our sleeves, demanding chewing gum, cigarettes, money. Skinny, they wore tattered clothes and appeared both hungry and bold. There was no getting away from them. Multitudes of aggressive, bony, brown hands tugged and clawed at us, pulling and pinching. Soon we were surrounded by a swarm of street urchins, who became more aggressive in their assaults. Then came the adults, cursing and shouting. Someone grabbed Charlie's bag from under his arm. He struggled as hands started to close in around him. What had begun as suspicion became grim reality in just a matter of seconds, and we fought for our lives. Our clothing torn, our eyes wide with fear, we broke into a run with the screaming Arabs after us. In the mad dash, I got separated from Charlie and ducked into a narrow alley. In those few minutes, it had become night and the alley was a dark tunnel.

Here and there a light appeared in a window. I noticed one a short distance ahead and thought it might be an inn or a store. Breathlessly I ran up a few steps and banged on the door, from under which stole a stream of light. In a moment the door opened, and I saw before me a scene resembling the Last Supper.

There was a festive aura radiating from the room, which was filled with people sitting around a long table partaking of a meal. Gasping for air, I tried to explain in my fractured French what my situation was. They smiled at me and, without questioning, as if they had expected me all along, led me to a vacant chair at the table. I sat down and joined a Jewish family in the celebration of a Passover seder. They sheltered me that night and, the next day, escorted me safely back to my ship.

RETURN

A feeling of adventure always pervaded the atmosphere on a tramp ship like ours. There was no telling till the last moment where our next harbor would be. And so it happened that, just before leaving Istanbul, news came that we would be going home to Poland. There was a cargo of cement waiting for us in Bone, Algeria, to be picked up on the way.

Once we knew we were going home, the Polish members of the crew started saving coffee, tea and sugar for our starved-out, survivors-of-the-war families. In Algiers we purchased all the foodstuffs we could get. I bought a duffel bag and filled it with carefully selected oranges, as well as chocolate, candy and clothing. It had been almost seven years since I left my country. I was approaching my 24th birthday.

ESCAPE INTO DANGER

It was a beautiful day in May when I steered the *Bialystok* into the port of Gdansk. I was the best helmsman on the ship and proud of it. Whenever we entered a new harbor and took a pilot on board to direct us, I was the one called on to take the wheel. I knew what cargo our ship carried, how heavy she was and how she would respond.

This time she was very heavy, with the cement, and it took her a while to turn. As we approached the harbor, the pilot came on board. I echoed his orders as we negotiated several shipwrecks at the port's entrance. Soon we were heading straight for the pier. I knew the ship wouldn't be able to turn in time, but I also knew I was to blindly obey the pilot's orders. Only the captain had the authority to change them. I glanced worriedly at the captain, who, suddenly perceiving the imminent danger, yelled out, "Starboard hard!" and threw the lever of the engine telegraph to full astern. The ship shuddered at this unexpected maneuver and slowed down, but nevertheless her bow was still headed straight for the pier. We only had 10 yards, and I gasped as we plowed into solid concrete.

Fortunately, the damage that occurred was over the water line. I hate to think what would have happened if water had entered the cement-laden holds!

WHAT MY PARENTS TOLD ME

As soon as we tied the ship to the pier, a throng of hungry people crowded aboard. They had risked their lives scavenging in mined fortifications for cameras, binoculars and small arms, and now they wanted to trade these treasures with the crew for canned food, sugar and coffee.

I stepped ashore and stared at the rubble and devastation. Gdansk was like an open wound. The ruins of buildings gaped with the black holes of burned-out windows. Here and there entire walls had collapsed, vividly exposing the guts of the expired life inside. One could still see family pictures hanging crookedly on the few remaining walls, or part of a dining room with shattered china still on a table, its legs dangling precariously over an upper floor precipice. The remnants of a tablecloth flapped in the wind and seemed to be sending a desperate message: *Look what you did! People lived here!*

Everywhere chaos reigned, and so did crime, greed and hunger. Russian soldiers, patrolling the cities and countryside, confiscated anything of value and often killed those unwilling to comply with their orders. That's why I carried a revolver, which I had traded for a pound of coffee. After so many narrow escapes, my life was very precious to me, and I longed to see my family.

The trains were manned by amateurs and ran very infrequently. I managed to climb into the freight car of one going in my direction and, once inside, sat on my luggage, carefully guarding between my knees the duffel bag full of oranges. By early morning I arrived at the last stop, the destroyed bridge over the Varta River. The train came to a halt in a field, and I got off with a handful of passengers. Then the train chugged away in the opposite direction.

It was quiet there among the tall grasses sprinkled with wildflowers. I could hear birds singing and the buzzing of insects. A young boy with a bicycle approached. "Take your baggage, sir?" he asked.

"Great!" I exclaimed. "Do you know the old schoolhouse in Bogdanovo?" Sure, he knew it. It was only a couple of kilometers away, he said, loading my gear on his bike. Then we both walked down the familiar road.

Seemingly not much had changed there during the years of war. This was farmland, with little villages sleeping among the meadows.

It was a short walk to the schoolhouse where my parents still lived and taught, but every step contained the memories of my childhood. How many times had I run through these paths between tall wheat fields? I wondered. Now I was a grown man, a survivor, looking for my footprints of yesterday.

From far away I saw the building among the clusters of lilac and jasmine. It was still early morning when I tipped the boy and opened the gate to the yard. My heart pounded with excitement on hearing the old creaking sound of the rusty hinges, the sound I recalled so many times in my dreams of coming home. It finally had come true!

I peered into a window and saw my father washing. As if suddenly hearing something, he looked up. An expression of disbelief came over his face. I heard him shout excitedly for my mother, and a moment later we were all in each other's arms, sobbing with happiness.

My mother held me at arm's length, eagerly looking at me. "My little boy, thank God you've finally come home," she cried. She repeated it over and over again, her lips trembling and her eyes filled with tears. She looked much older. Her hair had turned gray, and her face was very thin and etched with hunger and grief. Yet her eyes shone with love and life, as they always had.

My father had grayed, also. His sweeping black mustache, which I remembered so well, was now intertwined with many silver hairs. His gaunt face bore the signs of the war's ravages. Yet his smile was the same as I remembered. He didn't smile often, but when he did, everything around him seemed to change from darkness to light.

I spilled the contents of my duffel bag on the kitchen table—the oranges, chocolates, canned goods. My parents looked on with disbelief as I choked with pleasure at playing Santa Claus.

"Where is Marysia, and how is she?" I inquired of my younger sister.

"She's fine. We expect her here tomorrow," my mother said. "I guess you don't know that she is married."

It was hard for me to imagine my little sister married. "You already know about Viesia," my father said, pain suddenly contorting his face.

"Yes," I sighed. I realized this was the first time I had been able to talk about her since that day in England when I read my uncle's letter informing me of her death. I had been so shocked that I couldn't accept her loss. "You have to tell me all about her," I insisted. "I need to know everything that happened."

"We'll talk this evening," my father said wearily. "But now we have to go to the classrooms, to the children."

Indeed, I heard the calling and shouting of the children outside in the schoolyard. "Yes," I said, hugging them. "We'll talk all night. But now, I'll sleep." And I collapsed on a dilapidated old sofa while my parents, across the hallway, gently closed the doors to the two classrooms behind them.

The sleep I needed so badly was without dreams. Yet it was pervaded by a rich feeling of fulfillment. Like a ship returning from a long voyage to its home harbor, like a bird coming back to its nest, I felt like a marathon runner who, exhausted, finally reaches the finish line. I had a good feeling about the safe ending, and yet a dark shadow loomed between me and the sunlight. It was the death of my sister in the last days of the war.

I remember Viesia as a tall, frail girl with sad, dark brown eyes. It is difficult for me to describe why I loved her so much. I guess there was something very kind and good about her, something very gentle. She was not pretty, but I always thought she was beautiful.

Viesia meant the world to me. She was my inspiration and pride. As a teen-ager, and four years older than I, she was already an accomplished pianist, especially of Chopin's music. She fascinated me with her great ability to draw and paint. She was a brilliant scholar.

My younger sister, Marysia, whom I loved dearly and who had fine assets of her own, did not shine in the same way. I remember escorting Marysia through the "dangerous" peripheries of our village, bravely holding her hand. She looked up to me, probably in the same way I looked up to Viesia. I was not considered to be as intelligent or creative as Viesia, who overshadowed both Marysia and me.

Viesia was gentle with me and respected me.

There's no doubt that she was proud of me. "And this is my brother, Yurek. He is an artist," she would say as she introduced me to her high school friends. My budding ego unfolded and grew.

Viesia broke all scholastic records and had no difficulty getting into medical school. Yet she often didn't feel well and looked pale and sickly. Nobody ever told Marysia and me that Viesia was fighting tuberculosis. There were secrets kept from us younger children. I remember whisperings and serious talks behind closed doors. Our parents did everything they could to prevent Marysia and me from contracting the disease while protecting us from the knowledge of the danger that Viesia was in.

We saw very little of her during her medical studies at the University of Poznan. Then, two months before the Nazi invasion of Poland, I was about to embark on my training trip to South America. A few days before my departure, I saw Viesia for the last time.

It was a hot and humid July day in Gdynia. I managed to get liberty. Viesia had a summer job as a medical assistant at a children's camp nearby. We met and wandered about the town. I treated her to an ice cream. At 17, I tried to appear very grown up. Viesia cooperated and complimented me on my fancy Academy uniform.

"Do you remember the dreaming game I taught you to play when you were little?" she asked me as the time of our parting grew near. Of course I remembered how she taught me to cast a wishing spell and then how to watch the dream come true with the eyes of my mind. "You are leaving on a long voyage," she said, "and you'll be far away from us. Whenever you feel lonely, just cast the wish spell and we'll all be together again." She looked at me with her big dark eyes and smiled. We talked and joked and promised to write. Then we hugged good-bye, little knowing that this would be the last time we would ever see each other.

The war swept through Poland, leaving death and

destruction in its wake. Viesia wrote many letters to me at the Spanish concentration camp. She wrote about her work in a hospital where she was a medical assistant, about her everyday activities and chores, about the piano lessons she taught to the children of a well-to-do family. She even wrote that one day she had eaten ice cream and thought of me, wishing she could share it with me. Her letters were full of love and concern. From our separate corners of the world we watched the war ending, thinking of our reunion, planning our futures . . . .

I woke up and saw my mother looking at me. In a moment, everything came into focus. There I was, finally, back home.

That evening my parents and I sat near the old kerosene lamp. "You should have seen the surprise on the faces of my little ones," my mother said, "when I gave them the oranges you brought. They've never seen an orange before. They thought they were tomatoes. Poor children," she sighed, "they've suffered such hunger and neglect."

As she spoke, I watched her sunken face and saw deep, dark hollows around her eyes. Yet they still shone with love and compassion. To her, all children were her own.

She gave away all the oranges I had so carefully carried from North Africa! I thought. How could she? Didn't she want anything for herself? Then I realized that this must be the way my mother took in nourishment. By giving to others.

"Please tell me everything about Viesia," I said. "I must know how she died." I knew that what I was asking of my parents was very painful for them. It was opening a deep wound. Yet they realized how much it meant to me, so they told me the whole story. It was a story of pain, fear, desperation, love, compassion and deprivation.

This is what I learned from them. As the war was reaching its end, the people of Warsaw had risen up against their Nazi oppressors. But after months of bloody battles, outnumbered and ill-equipped, the insurgents were being methodically exterminated by German troops.

All month long January's cold wind had kept blowing the stench of burnt bodies and smoldering ashes as heavy German guns spewed their incendiary missiles into the ruins of Warsaw. Meanwhile, on the other side of the Vistula River, the Soviet army had watched and waited. They had stopped their offensive drive against the Germans, allowing the Nazis to slaughter the Warsaw insurgents. They had watched and waited because they hated the Poles as much as the Nazis.

Across the river from Warsaw, in a little hospital helplessly pinned between the German and Soviet armies, lay my sister Viesia. Her bed was a shabby cot in a room where a sharp, cold wind blew in through cracks in the dirty windows. At times a rat would saunter through a pile of rubbish in the corner.

In spite of the drafty room, Viesia had not felt cold. She was being consumed by fever, which left an unnatural blush over her pale, sunken face. Somewhere in the deep, dark hollows, her eyes had burned with a strange fire.

She knew she was dying. Time after time a painful cough had wracked her emaciated body, and blood had reddened the sputum on her parched lips. My mother and Viesia's husband had stayed at her side. With food supplies meager, having been plundered by the Germans and cut off by the blockade, there had been absolutely nothing to eat. One evening my father had come with a piece of bread that he had managed to trade for on a street corner.

In spite of her condition, Viesia had made little gifts for all of us. She had sewn and embroidered little flowers on scraps of velvet ribbon. "This one is for Yurek," she had said. "Please tell him when he comes back that I always loved him very much!"

Toward the end, she could hardly breathe. She had

said it felt like a knife was twisting in her lungs. Her suffering had been acute.

"Please, someone," she had whispered, "give me morphine! I cannot hold out any longer! Oh, God! Please stop this. Please . . . let me die!"

"I love you all" had been her last words. Then she had choked with a shattering cough and lay still. Only a narrow red ribbon of blood had oozed slowly from the corner of her mouth. The family had sighed with relief. All their tears had been drained in the last days of the death watch. They had sobbed, but their eyes had been dry.

Night came and darkness had closed in on a small group of people walking across a frozen stretch of the river. Their thin, gaunt figures with heads sadly lowered was etched darkly against the frequently illuminated sky over Warsaw. Though the weight of the cargo was light indeed, a skeletal horse had strained and occasionally slipped as it pulled a small cart carrying a simple coffin. In it my sister's body was returning home to be buried in a suburb of Warsaw.

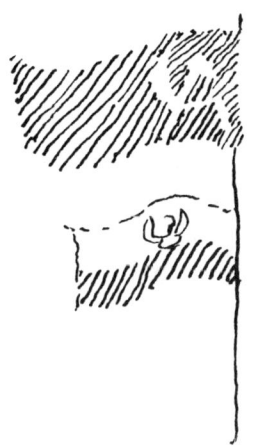

WRITING ON THE WALL

After a few days at home, I had to report back to the ship, which was in drydock for repairs. When I arrived there, I found out that we who had been fighting for Poland outside her borders were now considered undesirables by the current regime. The present Polish government called us the spoiled children of capitalism and claimed we had been directed by a fascist provisional-government-in-exile in London. We would probably make one more trip, after which we would be replaced by a crew of "true Poles," those who had established themselves in the protective wing of the Soviet Union's Communism.

I could see the handwriting on the wall. And when I learned that a political officer was being added to the crew, I knew yet another escape would be in order for me. Meanwhile, I was still a crew member and we would soon make our ship sea ready for a voyage to New York.

ANOTHER ESCAPE?

My sister Marysia was only 13 when the Nazis invaded Poland. Even at that young age, she was already involved in subversive activities against the Germans. As a courier for the Polish Underground, she was very brave. There were times when she carried weapons or patriotic leaflets. If she had been caught with them, she would have been shot on the spot. Once during a Nazi roundup of civilians, she *was* carrying leaflets. She had the courage to talk her way out of the situation and avoid being searched. She eventually met a young Polish cavalry officer who was a leader of a local guerrilla group. Janek fell in love with her, and they were married.

Now back home, as I looked at my sister, I saw she was not a silly teen-ager anymore. She had grown into a

ANOTHER ESCAPE

good-looking, gutsy woman. "We are in hiding," she explained to me. "Janek and I are both blacklisted by the present regime."

"But why?" I wanted to know. "You both fought Nazis, the common enemy."

"The Russians know that we are against Stalin's rule here," she explained. "We will have to leave Poland as soon as possible."

It became very clear to me that the Soviet Union would never permit Poland to stray from Communism.

At the beginning of the war, the Soviet Army had rounded up thousands of Polish officers in the woods of Katyn and, on special orders from Stalin, murdered them all, shooting each one individually with a bullet in the back of the head. Then the Russians buried the dead in a mass grave and planted trees over the whole area. Later, when accusations surfaced, the Russians blamed the Germans for the massacre. Evidently, Stalin thought that by eliminating the young officers, he would at least partially get rid of the anti-Communist opposition.

Poland had always been strategically important to the Soviet Union. I could foresee many rebellions against Soviet rule. The prisons would again be filled with patriotic Poles as they had been many times in the past. There would also be those who would leave Poland. Thinking about it, I realized that I would have to leave, too, and make my home in another country. I hoped it would be America. In a few days the *Bialystok* would be on her way to New York.

Poland was my home. It had taken me such a long time to return, only to have to leave it again.

A NEW BEGINNING

When the time came, I bade my family a poignant goodbye. With tears in my eyes, I embraced my parents and Marysia, thinking we might never see each other again. This was not the Poland I had known as a boy. My mother told me that every class had to start with a salute to Stalin. I knew I couldn't live here. I had suffered enough in the war and decided to break out at the first opportunity.

The political officer assigned to our ship was named Stefan Borski. He was a middle-aged, prematurely balding man, built like a wrestler. Through half-opened eyelids gleamed his spying eyes.

"The sonofabitch is writing secret notes about each of us," said my friend Stary one day as our ship sailed toward America. "You know, a political evaluation.

A NEW BEGINNING

Whatever you do, don't say a bad word about Stalin, because when you get back to Poland, they'll sure as hell throw you in the clink." I agreed, keeping to myself that I had no intention of going back.

Time passed at sea, and then one day we saw the New York skyline emerging from the mist. We entered the harbor and dropped anchor. To our left was the famous Statue of Liberty, and in front of us skyscrapers blinked with a thousand eyes. At that moment I knew I was going to live here. But how? Obviously, I could jump ship and lose myself in the city. But I knew that would be illegal and prevent me from ever becoming a U.S. citizen. Besides, I had very little money and didn't know anyone who could help me. Even my English was limited to just a few simple words.

But again, luck was with me. A few days after we docked, a water barge came alongside our ship to replenish our water supply. I heard some of the men speaking Polish and I asked them for advice. "There's a sure way you could become a citizen," one of them said. "Join the Army."

By then it was the summer of 1946. The air was as humid as in a Turkish bath, the heat oppressive. Trying to cool off, I stood in front of an electric fan and let blasts of cold air whip my body. Before long, I developed a sore throat and a head cold. (Someone joked that I should cough and sneeze on Borski.) Gradually a thought dawned on me: Why catch only a cold when, with a little effort, I could get pneumonia? That may sound cynical, but in my case it made sense.

After three days, I was down with such a high fever that the officer in charge of the ship's sickroom sent me to see our shipping company's doctor in the city. While sitting in the waiting room, I purposely smoked several cigarettes in succession to worsen my condition. As I expected, the doctor ordered me to be hospitalized immediately. Half dead, I returned to the ship for my gear. But I had enough presence of mind to obtain a bona fide medical discharge signed by the ship's first officer. "You're lucky Borski isn't around," Stary whispered. "He's probably in his cabin, the miserable bastard!" Borski had opposed my visit to the doctor and now would almost certainly try to confine me to the ship's sickroom. But he didn't appear on the scene until it was too late. By that time I had already scrambled down the gangway and into a motorboat, and Stary had started the engine.

It was then that I saw Borski leaning over the rail, waving and screaming "Stop that man!" as he threw himself in helpless rage against the rail. *"I want that man back on board!"*

He wanted me, dead or alive, but what could he do? The roar of the motor drowned out his ranting. Holding the tiller with one hand, Stary grinned and waved back with the other, pretending not to hear. He had to pretend, knowing he'd have to face Borski on his return. As for me, I was ecstatic. Borski couldn't stop me now. I was on my way to start a new life in America. So, as we sped toward Staten Island Marine Hospital, I gave him the finger. I had the two things that would set me free: pneumonia and my medical discharge papers.

The sky was bright blue over Manhattan, and a little breeze kissed my face with salty spray. Far on my left, the Lady in the Harbor smiled at me.

EPILOGUE

It is now November 1992, and I am 70 years old, living with my wife, Iris, in a retirement community in Cranbury, NJ. We have four children and four grandchildren.

I left you, dear reader, in 1946. As you may recall, I was advised to join the U.S. Army. I did so, and subsequently was sent to Korea, where I served a very cold eight months. After my discharge, I realized my quest for U.S. citizenship. I returned to New York City, where I found employment as an artisan in the porcelain industry and studied art at night at the Art Students League of New York. I learned to speak English by reading *Gone with the Wind* from cover to cover with the help of a Polish-English dictionary. (In those days there was no television or Berlitz language schools.) A few years later, while working as a designer for Lenox China, I studied at the Academy of the Fine Arts in Philadelphia. When my daughter Stacy was born, I changed my name from Iwaszkiewicz toIvers because I wanted to spare her the ribbing I had often encountered, *i.e.*, being referred to at Army mail call as "George Alphabet."

Gradually over the years I gained recognition as a painter, sculptor and printmaker. My artwork was chosen three times by UNICEF for its holiday greeting card collections—in 1970, 1984 and 1990. I have participated in many art shows and have won numerous awards. My work is in the collections of the Brooklyn Museum, the Jewish Museum of New York, the Art Museum of Princeton University, the New Jersey State Museum, Worcester College Museum in England, the art museums of Torun, Bydgoszcz and Grudziadz, Poland, the Vatican, and many private collections. Among the galleries that carry my work are the Sandpiper Galerie, Stone Harbor, NJ; Nica Gallery, Pullman, WA; and Cranbury Station Art Gallery, Princeton, NJ.

I have had a rich life but, unfortunately, 11 years ago I developed Parkinson's Disease, a progressive disorder of the central nervous system. Despite this, I am still doing my artwork. There is so much more to learn and to experience. In a way, my artwork is my last escape, this time from the pain and indignities of my illness.

For me, though, life is still precious.